THEORY INTO PRACTICE

This is the second publication in the series
"Collected Writings of the Orpheus Institute"
edited by Peter Dejans

THEORY INTO PRACTICE

Composition, Performance and the Listening Experience

Nicholas Cook
Peter Johnson
Hans Zender

COLLECTED WRITINGS OF THE

ORPHEUS

INSTITUTE

Leuven University Press
1999

CONTENTS

PREFACE / P. 6

TEXTS

— Nicholas Cook
Words about Music, or Analysis Versus Performance / P. 9

— Peter Johnson
Performance and the Listening Experience:
Bach's "Erbarme Dich" / P. 55

— Hans Zender
A Roadmap for Orpheus?
About Non-Linear Codes of Music for the Descent into its Underworld / P. 103

PERSONALIAE / P. 118

COLOFON / P. 120

PREFACE

Theory Into Practice: Composition, Performance and the Listening Experience is the second publication in the *Writings of the Orpheus Institute* series.

Like the first publication, *Inter Disciplinas Ars*, the articles in this book are the result of presentations held during the annual seminar of the Orpheus Institute at Château de la Rocq in Arquennes, in November 1998. The central theme of this conference was the relationship between the reflection about and the realisation of a musical composition.

In his paper *Words About Music, or Analysis versus Performance*, Nicholas Cook states that words and music can never be aligned exactly with one another, that there is always a remainder, a non-linearity in the mapping of what is said onto what is played. Cook embarks on a quest for models of the relationship between analytical conception and performance that are more challenging (both intellectually and musically) than those in general currency.

It is precisely this 'performance analysis' that also constitutes the starting point for Peter Johnson's article *Performance and The Listening Experience: Bach's "Erbarme dich"*. He shows that a performance is an element within the intentionality of the work itself and as such a central factor in the ontology of the work. Identifying the artistic contents of a performance is a major point of his paper: based on spectrogram analyses, he compares two performances of Bach's aria "Erbarme dich" in order to show that recent methods of music theory manage to interpret a performance's subjective reception in an objective way.

The composer Hans Zender, in his *A Road Map for Orpheus? About Non-Linear Codes of Music For The Descent Into Its Underworld*, talks about generally accepted axioms in our compositional *poiesis*. A composer must be capable of questioning obvious basic principles (such as equal temperament) and finding creative solutions, or at least identify alternatives and allow his findings to guide his artistic decisions. In the second part of his text, Zender illustrates his statements by means of some of his own works.

Given that the original presentations were given in the English and German languages, we decided to publish this book in both English and Dutch (ISBN 90 6186 993 5). If you'd like to receive Hans Zender's original German text via e-mail, do not hesitate to contact us.

I would like to thank my co-editor Frank Agsteribbe as well as all people who, in one way or another, contributed to this publication.

Peter Dejans

WORDS ABOUT MUSIC,
OR ANALYSIS VERSUS PERFORMANCE

Nicholas Cook

WORDS ABOUT WORDS ABOUT MUSIC

To anyone who takes exception to the title of this paper, the section title must seem worse. For musicians are perenially suspicious of words, seeing them as a means not so much of clarification as of obfuscation; if there is anything worse than words about music, I hear you saying, it must be words about words (about music).

But there is something paradoxical about this musicianly suspicion of words — something reminiscent of Borges's account of the traveller Abulcasim Al-Ashari, who claimed to have been to China but whose detractors, "with that peculiar logic of hatred, swore that he had never set foot in China and that in the temples of that land he had blasphemed the name of Allah".[1] For on the one hand we complain that words can't represent music, that they distort and even betray an art whose essence lies in its evanescence, lending it a spurious and domesticating determinacy while at the same time being vague (as Felix Mendelssohn put it) just where music is precise. But on the other hand we try to use words to do just what we say they can't do, that is to represent music — to stand in for it, in the manner of a working model or a simulacrum. We claim that music cannot be translated into words, but at the same time we expect them to say how it is. Under these circumstances it is hardly surprising if we find that, when we talk about music, we never quite say what we mean or mean what we say; to put it another way, it seems impossible to talk about music without finding that you have inadvertently changed the subject.

The problem is not that words are inadequate for music, but that we tend to have unreasonable expectations of them. And when they do not fulfil these expectations — when we conclude

---

1. Jorge Luis Borges, "Averroes' Search", in: *Labyrinths: Selected Stories and Other Writings*. New York 1964, p. 150.

that the gap between words and music is unbridgeable — we seek to devalue them, hurrying through the words so as to get to the music with the minimum delay (for isn't a phrase of music, like a picture, worth a thousand words?). It is like the premature 'rush to interpretation' which Richard Middleton condemns in sociologically-inclined writers on popular music,[2] only the other way round: where the sociologists explain meaning without exploring the musical properties that support it, musicians rush from words to music without attending sufficiently to the conditions of their signification. But in truth the requisite rethinking of words about music need not take long. For it stands to reason that if words cannot say what music says, our purpose in deploying them must be to say what music does not say. Or to put it less paradoxically, the way we talk about music does not simply replicate it (if that were the case, words about music really would be redundant) but rather affects the way we make it, not to mention what we make *of* it. Words change what we play and what we hear. It is precisely because words do not just stand in for music that they matter so much: a musical tradition is as much as anything a historically transmitted way of talking about music.

The issue of words about music penetrates to the core of music's cultural identity, but is particularly pressing in relation to its performance. It would be hard to think of another area in which musicology (etymologically 'words about music') has been so conspicuously at odds with cultural practice; the whole thrust of scholarly writing about music has until recently been to downplay the variance between one performance and another, so locating the aesthetic centre of music in the written text. Under such circumstances the performer's highest legitimate aspiration becomes one of adequacy, of acting as an ideally transparent medium between composer and audience without the intrusion of his or her own personality; it was said of Hans von Bülow that when you heard him play Beethoven you had no sense of Bülow's presence but only of Beethoven's, and such remarks, indicative of high praise, continue to be made of performers to this day. (The other side of the coin is expressed in Schoenberg's famous if ironical dic-

---

2. Richard Middleton, *Studying Popular Music*. Milton Keynes 1990, p. 220.

tum that "the performer, for all his intolerable arrogance, is totally unnecessary except as his interpretations make the music understandable to an audience unfortunate enough not to be able to read it in print".[3]) And for their part, performers have tended to see words as less a means of engagement with music than one of deferral; there is a widespread suspicion of musicological pronouncements about performance, in particular those that advocate a particular performance practice on the basis of structural analysis. Even as analytically informed a performer as Alfred Brendel has said that "few analytical insights have a direct bearing on performance, and that analysis should be the outcome of an intimate familiarity with the piece rather than an input of established concepts".[4]

Yet in no other area of musical activity is it quite so literally true that what we say determines what we do; after all, conservatory teachers may be hired for what they play but they are paid for what they say. If many of their students would nevertheless sign up to Elvis Costello's contemptuous dismissal of the value of words about music,[5] that is because of the pervasive assumption that words should do what they cannot do: stand in for music, replicate it. In this paper I argue that words and music can never be aligned exactly with one another, that there is always a remainder, a non-linearity in the mapping of what is said onto what is played. In short, you can't play it as you say it. But if we can tease apart the saying and the playing, the words and the music, then two benefits may follow. It may be possible to develop models of the relationship between analytical conception and performance that are more challenging (both intellectually and musically) than those in general currency. And this in turn may facilitate the devel-

---

3. Quoted in Dika Newlin, *Schoenberg Remembered: Diaries and Recollections (1938–76)*. New York 1980, p. 164. How literally Newlin's recollections should be assumed to reflect what Schoenberg actually said is a moot point (I owe this observation to Peter Johnson).
4. Alfred Brendel, *Music Sounded Out: Essays, Lectures, Interviews, Afterthoughts*. London 1990, p. 249.
5. In an interview Costello remarked that "writing about music is like dancing about architecture. It's a really stupid thing to want to do". But according to Robert Walser, Thelonius Monk said it first ("The Body in the Music: Epistemology and Musical Semiotics", in: *College Music Symposium* 31 (1991), pp. 117–126).

opment of what is coming to be known as 'performance studies': a musicological subdiscipline which accords to the performance and the performer some of the serious interest previously reserved for the score and its composer. All this, of course, adds up to an agenda that goes way beyond what can be accomplished in this paper. But that is no reason for not making a start.

WORDS ABOUT PERFORMANCE

Maybe I have drawn too strong a line between musicologists and performers. After there, all there are those, particularly in the area of historical musicology, who have distinguished themselves on both sides of the line (Charles Rosen is the outstanding example). The real gap, then, lies not between individuals but activities: writing about music and playing it. All the same, when it comes to analysis it is possible to distinguish between two literary genres, one associated with writers who play and the other with players who write. When people speak of analysis and performance, it is generally the former to which they refer: writings by professional analysts and theorists which attempt to establish some kind of linkage between the structure of music and its performance, and which are in some cases explicitly directed at the performer. But there is another literature, though rarely recognized as such, which is the work of professional performers, and which is best represented by Alfred Brendel's books. In *Musical Thoughts and Afterthoughts*,[6] Brendel puts forward a model of musical structure which he regards as indispensable for the performer of Beethoven's piano sonatas, and which he terms 'foreshortening'. (Without entering into details, the idea is that any significant structural point in the music is preceded by a series of phrases of diminishing length; it is by articulating these phrase-lengths that the performer can do justice to the musical structure.) And while it is not particularly obvious for whom the book is written, it is evident that theorists are included among the target readership, for Brendel explains that he has been unable to develop the concept of foreshortening to the full, and explicitly invites "colleagues

---

6. Alfred Brendel, *Musical Thoughts and Afterthoughts*. London 1976.

whose time is less limited than my own" — presumably the theorists — to undertake this task.[7]

What makes Brendel's concept of foreshortening typical of what might be termed the literature of 'performers' analysis' is its summary nature.[8] By this I mean two things. In the first place the concept of foreshortening, and the identification of structural points which it supports, gives rise a framework that is intended to coordinate all the parameters of performance variance (tempo, rhythm, dynamics, articulation, and so on); the assumption is that by internalizing this framework the performer will gain a degree of interpretive control otherwise impossible. And this idea of the summary framework links back to Rachmaninov's idea of the culminating moment or 'point' (if you missed the 'point', he said, your performance could never be articulate),[9] and forward to the graphical interpretations which John Rink has recently been proposing as a means of bridging the gap between analysis and performance. But the examples of Rachmaninov and Rink also illustrate the second way in which analyses that explicitly adopt the performer's perspective might be said to be summary. Rachmaninov never explained the basis on which the 'point' of a piece of music was to be established; his concept is theoretically undefined and therefore mysterious. (That is, it is 'summary' in the sense that no evidence or rationalization is provided.) And while Rink is himself a professional theorist, his graphs are open to criticism on rather similar grounds.

A representative example is the graph of Liszt's "Vallée d'Obermann" in Rink's article "Translating Musical Meaning".[10] It looks like the increasingly familiar graphs that plot tempo

---

7. Ibidem, p. 9.
8. For a review of this literature see Jennifer Tong, *Separate Discourses: A Study of Performance and Analysis*. PhD diss., University of Southampton 1994, chapter 4.
9. Harold Schonberg, *The Great Pianists*. London 1964, p. 368.
10. John Rink, "Translating Musical Meaning: The Nineteenth-century Performer as Narrator", in: Nicholas Cook and Mark Everist (eds.), *Rethinking Music*. Oxford 1999, pp. 217–238, especially fig. 10.2 (p. 236). As explained in notes 67–68 of his chapter, Rink adapted his notion of the intensity curve from Wallace Berry, who however used it as a purely analytical device rather than as a representation of performance; Rink also draws parallels with the work of Neil Todd (see n. 83 below) and Manfred Clynes.

deviation against time, but in fact represents a variable which Rink terms 'intensity'. By this he does not mean intensity in the physical sense, nor indeed any other objectively determinable attribute of either the music or its performance. What he offers is rather "a graphic representation of the music's ebb and flow, its 'contour' in time, determined by all active elements (harmony, melody, rhythm, dynamics, etc.) working either independently, in synchrony, or out of phase with one another to create the changing degrees of energy and thus the overall shape".[11] But there are no rules for assessing the relative contribution of these elements, which means that "an intensity curve relies upon the analyst/performer's musical judgements".[12] This, Rink admits, creates a problem: "the difficulty of defining and objectively quantifying intensity". And if there are no explicit rules for deriving intensity values from the score, then the same applies to the application of the intensity curve to performance, for there is no implication that it is to be directly translated into, say, tempo or dynamic variation. Nevertheless, Rink claims, the construct is powerful from the performer's point of view; like Brendel's foreshortening structure, once internalized it can act as a coordinating framework for performance. Accordingly Rink links his intensity curve not only with the unsystematized but ubiquitous gestural representations that characterize music lessons and rehearsals, but also with historical concepts of performance (he cites in particular the *grande ligne* of nineteenth-century commentators).

The problem with Rink's intensity curves, as I see it, is that they are insufficiently grounded in analytical method. This is not the same as complaining that they have no objective existence; that, after all, could be said of many of the most familiar analytical constructs, for (as Matthew Brown and Douglas Dempster have expressed it) "it is not in the least bit clear what sort of entity a middleground, or an implied dominant, or a nexus set might conceivably be".[13] It is rather a matter of intersubjectivity, of having

---

11. Ibidem, p. 234.
12. Ibidem, p. 235 n. 68.
13. Matthew Brown and Douglas J. Dempster, "The Scientific Image of Music Theory", in: *Journal of Music Theory* 33 (1989), pp. 65–106, especially p. 97.

established if informal discovery procedures that enable different individuals to reproduce the identification of a particular analytical construct. This in turn is a question of experiencing or (as musicians say) 'hearing' the music in a particular way; as Marion Guck puts it, "when analysts write analytical texts, we are offering readers the possibility of recreating a hearing that we have found worthwhile".[14] And the role of an analytical method is to support the hearing through a demonstration that is as much practical as logical. The problem with Rink's intensity curves, then, is in essence the same as with Rachmaninov's 'point' (and even, arguably, with Brendel's foreshortening):[15] there is no way in which the reader, or performer, can disassemble the contribution of the various musical parameters to the summary graph and so reconstruct the experience of the music that motivates it. As a result the analysis has no greater explanatory value than would a performance that embodied it.

The work of Rink, then, represents a concerted and indeed unique attempt on the part of a theorist to adopt a performer's perspective, but he only achieves his goal to the extent that he severs his links with theory. In this way he does not so much create a bridge between analysis and performance as simply cross from the one terrain to the other. The prevailing picture in the field of analysis and performance, however, is exactly the reverse: theoretically legitimate interpretations whose application to performance remains problematic. The principal example of such as approach is Wallace Berry, whose book *Musical Structure and Performance* was more than anything responsible for establishing the subdiscipline of performance studies.[16] Berry was not only a professional

---

14. Marion Guck, "The 'Endless Round'", in: *Perspectives of New Music* 31 (1993), pp. 306–314, especially p. 307; cited and commented upon in her chapter "Rehabilitating the Incorrigible", in: Anthony Pople (ed.), *Theory, Analysis and Meaning in Music*. Cambridge 1994, pp. 57–73. Guck also describes analyses as a "medium of intersubjective exchange".
15. Jennifer Tong illustrates the largely arbitrary nature of Brendel's application of the foreshortening principle in "Separate Discourses", p. 154FF.
16. Wallace Berry, *Musical Structure and Performance*. New Haven 1989. The following discussion is in part condensed from Nicholas Cook, "Analysing Performance, and Performing Analysis", in: Nicholas Cook and Mark Everist (eds.), *Rethinking Music*, pp. 239–261.

theorist but also an accomplished pianist and conductor, and his book is full of insights regarding ways in which structural relationships can be projected (or 'brought out', as musicians say) in performance; under certain circumstances he also advocated what he called a 'neutral' style of performance, that is to say one in which the performer explicitly refrains from inflecting the music towards one structural interpretation or another. But there is an essential inflexibility in his way of thinking about the relationship between analysis and performance. The basic trouble is that he sees it as a one-way relationship. So he speaks of "the path from analysis to performance" (elsewhere enlarged to "the path from analysis to interpretive decision"), and describes the central topic of his book as "how (...) a structural relation exposed in analysis can be illuminated in the inflections of edifying performance".[17] In other words, you begin by analyzing and end by performing; the one leads to the other.

To be fair to Berry, in seeing the relationship of analysis and performance in this way he was only repeating well-established views expressed, for example, by Rudolf Kolisch ("only when one has reached the point where one feels completely certain of how the piece must go should the realization process commence")[18] and Benjamin Britten ("after the intellect has finished work, the instinct must take over. In performance the analysis must be forgotten.")[19] One might object that the relationship between writing (or reading) and playing is not so simple, that it is less like a sequence and more like a counterpoint; Glenn Gould surely spoke for many performers when he claimed that "the ideal way to go about making a performance (...) is to assume that when you begin, you don't quite know what it is about. You only come to know as you proceed."[20] But what is of perhaps greater significance is the way in which, as is so often the case, a claim of

---

17. Berry, *Musical Structure and Performance*, pp. 10, 2, x. I shall not on this occasion explore the ramifications of that interesting word 'edifying'.
18. Paraphrased by Joan Allen Smith in *Schoenberg and his Circle: A Viennese Portrait*. New York 1986, p. 106.
19. Foreword to Erwin Stein, *Form and Performance*. London 1962, p. 8.
20. Tim Page (ed.), *The Glenn Gould Reader*. London 1987, p. 287; cited and discussed in Jonathan Dunsby, *Performing Music: Shared Concerns*. Oxford 1995, pp. 39, 46.

chronological priority slips imperceptibly into an asserted hierarchy of authority. In Berry's book this hierarchy is implicit rather than explicit; it resides in the simple fact that the book is written by a theorist and takes the form of injunctions to performers, providing no occasion for the reciprocal process — for the theorist to learn from performers, that is to say. (In fact, as Joel Lester has pointed out, there is a striking omission from the entire literature of which Berry's book is representative: 'performers and their performances'.[21]) But other theorists have promulgated the hierarchical relationship between themselves and performers quite explicitly, and none more so than than Eugene Narmour in his article "On the Relationship of Analytical Theory to Performance and Interpretation".

One of the passages on which Narmour focusses is taken from Act 2, Scene 1 of Richard Strauss's *Der Rosenkavalier* — the moment when Sophie falls in love as she accepts Octavian's silver rose.[22] Narmour begins by analyzing the passage on the basis of his customary implication-realization model, arguing that the otherworldly effect of the music (matching the words "how heavenly, not earthly") arises from the way in which, as he puts it, "practically every melodic event is in some way unexpected and in some way unclosed".[23] For instance, he observes that Strauss marks the $a\#^2$ on 'himmlische' *pianissimo*, whereas the ascent of a sixth from the preceding $c\#^1$ might have been expected to give rise to a *crescendo*. Again, the leap to $a\#^2$ creates the expectation of a descent within the intervallic area defined by the leap, whereas just the opposite happens: the melody rises to b^2. And for Narmour this has a clear performance implication: "a *further* reduction in dynamic on the unexpected step up to the dissonant, syncopated, high B will also be extremely affective in an aesthetic sense".[24] On

---

21. Joel Lester, "Performance and Analysis: Interaction and Interpretation", in: John Rink (ed.), *The Practice of Performance: Studies in Musical Interpretation*. Cambridge 1995, pp. 197–216, especially p. 197.
22. Eugene Narmour, "On the Relationship of Analytical Theory to Performance and Interpretation", in: Eugene Narmour and Ruth Solie (eds.), *Explorations in Music, the Arts, and Ideas: Essays in Honor of Leonard B. Meyer*. Stuyvesant 1988, pp. 317–340.
23. Ibidem, p. 332.
24. Ibidem, p. 333.

the basis of this and similar arguments, Narmour ends up with what he describes as "an analytically justifiable recreative interpretation" of the passage, which he presents in the form of an annotated score.[25] He then works through a series of commercial recordings to see how well they match up. The Karajan recording, with Teresa Stich-Randall, turns out to be a clear best buy.

There are two particularly striking characteristics of Narmour's approach. One is the way in which the theorist is set up as the arbiter of performance. This is built into the very procedure that Narmour adopts, with his derivation of an analytical model against which recorded performances are assessed for compliance. It pervades his rhetoric, too, for he frequently refers to what performers 'must' or 'must not' do. Again, referring to a passage from Haydn's Symphony No. 83, he observes that Leonard Bernstein makes 'an obvious mistake', while Julius Katchen's handling of motives is 'inexplicable'. And at one point Narmour's exasperation boils over: "Sometimes", he snorts, "conductors do utterly inexplicable things which make no sense at all".[26] The implication is plain: what performers do is either capable of theoretical explanation, or else it is wrong. There could hardly be a starker contrast with the respectful language which theorists use for composers, or a clearer expression of the performer's place at the bottom of academic-music pecking order.[27] But the second characteristic to which I referred is perhaps the more important: the directness with which Narmour moves from analysis to performance interpretation. The right performance, he seems to imply, is the one that corresponds to the right analysis. Admittedly he shrinks from a direct statement that there can only be one ideal interpretation:

---

25. Ibidem, ex. 3.
26. Ibidem, p. 333.
27. A telling contrast is offered by Janet Schmalfeldt's article "On the Relation of Analysis to Performance: Beethoven's Bagatelles Op. 126, Nos. 2 and 5", in: *Journal of Music Theory* 29 (1985), pp. 1–31, which is cast in the form of a dialogue between two distinct authorial personas: the analyst and the performer. It has to be admitted that the relationship between them is not very equal, however; Joel Lester has pointed out that Schmalfeldt's "pianist-persona is learning to play the pieces, but it is obvious from her prose that her analyst-persona has studied them long and hard" ("Performance and Analysis", p. 198 n. 1). And the participants seem more inclined to lecture than to listen to one another (this applies in particular to the analyst, of course).

"in an art like music", he says, "there can never be any such thing as *the* definitive performance".²⁸ But he effectively negates this when he continues: "The point, however, is that, given the analytical theory applied in [the annotated score], we can say more or less objectively that (...) certain performances are subtly though demonstrably better than others". The professional 'we' immediately reinstates the theorist's authority and hence the hierarchy to which I have referred.

In this way the whole thrust of Narmour's thinking is to elide analytical and performance interpretation. Jonathan Dunsby, by contrast, begins to tease them apart when he writes that "A particular analysis may well lead to the conviction that a particular kind of interpretation is essential, but how to convey that interpretation to the listener in performance is a different matter".²⁹ Even if you regard one particular analytical interpretation as right, he is saying, that doesn't mean you can extrapolate one particular performance interpretation from it; any number of different performances might be capable of doing justice to the same analysis. And in saying this, Dunsby is making a distinction that can be traced back to Heinrich Schenker, and specifically to his 1912 monograph on Beethoven's Ninth Symphony. Schenker's groundbreaking book (which so impressed the conductor Wilhelm Furtwängler that he sought Schenker out and established a long-term professional relationship with him) takes the symphony section by section, analyzing the musical content and drawing conclusions for performance. But in his preface, Schenker is concerned to forestall an obvious objection: that his recommendations for performance are not infrequently opposed to Beethoven's notated directions. The contradiction is only apparent, Schenker explains. And he continues: "it is not the task of the orthography, as is generally believed and taught, to provide the

---

28. Narmour, "On the Relationship of Analytical Theory to Performance", p. 334. For a philosophical defence of interpretive pluralism in performance see Michael Krausz, "Rightness and Reasons in Musical Interpretation", in: Michael Krausz (ed.), *The Interpretation of Music: Philosophical Essays*. Oxford 1993, pp. 75–87.
29. Jonathan Dunsby, "Guest Editorial: Performance and Analysis of Music", in: *Music Analysis* 8 (1989), pp. 5–20, especially p. 7.

player with perfectly definite means for achieving effects allegedly specified and attainable only through precisely these means, but rather to arouse in his mind, in an a priori manner, specific effects, leaving it up to him to chose freely the appropriate means for their attainment".[30]

Schenker's language is perhaps obscure but his meaning is clear enough: in his score Beethoven's concern has been to notate the content of the symphony or, to put it another way, the intended musical effects. The purpose of the orthography (Schenker has in mind slurs, dynamic markings, and so forth) is to convey the effect to the performer. Once this has been achieved, the orthography has served its function; it is now up to the performer to decide through what technical means to create the effect that Beethoven intended.[31] In this way Schenker seems to return to performers some of the freedom that Narmour denies them.

But if the contradiction that Schenker wants to allay is apparent rather than real, so too is the freedom. Performers are free to decide on the technical means precisely because, and to the extent that, their decisions do not bear upon the aesthetic effect. Schenker is not according an interpretive role to performers in any aesthetically significant sense; in another context, in fact, he exclaims "No interpretation!" [32] The reason for this is that, as he puts it, "Performance must come from within the work; the work

---

30. Heinrich Schenker (John Rothgeb, transl. and ed.), *Beethoven's Ninth Symphony: A Portrayal of its Musical Content, with Running Commentary on Performance and Literature as well*. New Haven 1992, p. 9.

31. For a discussion of this issue see William Rothstein, "Heinrich Schenker as an Interpreter of Beethoven's Piano Sonatas", in: *19th-Century Music* 8 (1984), pp. 3-28, especially p. 10. Interestingly, Furtwängler made the same point: "a score cannot give the slightest clue as to the intensity of a forte or piano or exactly how fast a tempo should be (...). The dynamics are quite deliberately not literal but symbolic, not with a practical meaning for each individual instrument but of a broad significance, added with the sense of the work as a whole in mind". However Furtwängler appears to go beyond this to make the same direct identification of the right analysis and the right performance as Narmour: "for every musical work (...) there is only one approach, one manner of interpretation, that consistently proves to make the deepest impression, precisely because it is the 'correct' interpretation". See: R. Taylor (ed. and transl.), *Furtwängler on Music*. Aldershot 1991, pp. 8-9, 12.

32. From Schenker's unfinished "Entwurf einer 'Lehre vom Vortrag'", quoted and translated by Rothstein, "Heinrich Schenker as an Interpreter", p. 10.

must breathe from its own lungs — from the linear progressions, neighboring tones, chromatic tones, modulations (...). About these, naturally, there cannot exist different interpretations."[33] In this way the familiar pecking order is once more reinscribed, for the arbiter of interpretation is of course the theorist, who alone is in a position to speak to the linear progressions, neighbouring tones, and the rest. But the delimitation of the sphere of performance goes beyond this, for interpretation is simply removed from it. Schenker's position ends up little different from Narmour's: interpretation is either implicit in the work (in which case it is open to analytical explanation), or else it is wrong. We are back at the self-effacing presence, or rather absence, for which Bülow was praised when he played Beethoven. And if this seems a trifle ironic, bearing in mind Schenker's more or less vitriolic views of his fellow Beethoven-editor,[34] we can refer instead to Brahms's comments on performing Beethoven, which Schenker quoted with approbation: "When I play something of Beethoven, I have absolutely no individuality in relation to it; rather, I try to *reproduce* the piece as well as Beethoven wrote it. Then I have [quite] enough to do."[35]

The story of successive attempts to forge a meaningful relationship between analysis and performance could, of course, be told at greater length. In particular, the varied essays that comprise John Rink's edited volume *The Practice of Performance* represent a sustained attempt to get away from traditional ideas of performers 'bringing out' analytical structure and to identify some kind of middleground between music-theoretical discourse and performance; the hard edges that characterize, say, Narmour's position are softened, and entrenched assumptions questioned. For instance, Joel Lester explicitly focusses on the multiplicity of interpretational possibilities routinely offered by any piece of music, exploring the ways in which alternative analytical and performance interpretations may be mapped onto one another. Again,

---

33. Ibidem, combining two separate statements in the "Entwurf".
34. See Nicholas Cook, "The Editor and the Virtuoso, or Schenker versus Bülow", in: *Journal of the Royal Musical Association* 116 (1991), pp. 78–95.
35. Quoted and translated (from Schenker's *Erläuterungsausgabe* of Op. 110) in: Rothstein, "Heinrich Schenker as an Interpreter", p. 26 n. 13.

William Rothstein's contribution emphasizes how, given a particular structure, the performer may sometimes be called on to conceal rather than to project structure; it may be "better for the performer to suggest something which is 'false' — or more precisely, something which is 'true' only from a certain, partial vantage point — than to spell out everything one knows."[36] He also adds, using an illuminating analogy to which I shall return, that on such occasions "the performer adopts temporarily the viewpoint of one or two characters in the drama, so to speak, rather than assuming omniscience at every moment".

But the bridges between analysis and performance that are built by Rink's contributors are generally flimsy and temporary. They paper over an ideological gulf and in this sense are not supported by the available conceptual apparatus; they are victories snatched from the jaws of theoretical incoherence. And consequently we are left at the end more or less where we began: caught between Scylla and Charybdis. On the one side, the performer is subordinated to the theorist, with his or her freedom of action reduced to the aesthetically insignificant. Or on the other, as in the case of Rink's own writings, the analyst reaches a more genuine accommodation with the performer, but at the expense of what might be termed the epistemology that grounds any kind of analytical explanation. The situation, in short, bears all the hallmarks of a debate that is taking place within an inappropriately constrained conceptual framework, and we shall see that there are good historical reasons why this should be the case.

MULTIPLE AGENCIES

If we are to take seriously the contribution of performance to the aesthetic phenomenon of music, and more, if we are to theorize it, then it will be necessary to reconsider a number of the key concepts of traditional musicology (and not just musicology). Two of these are identifiable less as explicit assumptions than through a

---

36. William Rothstein, "Analysis and the Act of Performance", in: Rink, *The Practice of Performance*, pp. 217–240, especially p. 238.

widespread if untheorized resistance to thinking in terms of the opposite: the concept of the single musical work (as represented in the definitive version or *Urtext*), and that of undivided authorship. The third is represented by a conceptual model in which the author (composer) and listener are connected by a single line, with the performer occupying an intermediate position. All three have their origins in a common aesthetic ideology, but the third is the most deeply embedded and so I shall begin with the other two.

As I suggested, the concepts of the definitive version and of undivided authorship emerge most clearly through the attempt to cling to them against the odds. A particularly conspicuous example is provided by the strategies adopted during the early to mid-1990s by American music theorists concerned to bring the study of rock music within the purview of their discipline. Until the late 1980s or even after, rock music tended to be studied almost anywhere *except* in conservatories and university departments of music: that is, in departments of media studies, cultural studies, or sociology. And the result was, inevitably, that lyrics, commentaries, fandom, and material or economic infrastructure were prioritized at the expense of 'the primary text' (as Allan Moore styles it in the title of his book on progressive rock),[37] in other words, the music. In view of the persistence within the musical academy of connoisseur-based attitudes long eclipsed in other disciplines, it is hardly surprising that the apologists for rock music adopted what might be termed a conservative stance. Some took this strategy as far as to apply such canonic analytical methods as Schenkerian reduction to rock (the most thoroughgoing example of this trend is Walter Everett's work on the Beatles).[38] Others were methodologically more eclectic, but went to sometimes extraordinary lengths to fit rock into the established framework of music-

---

37. Allan F. Moore, *Rock: The Primary Text*. Buckingham 1993.
38. See for Walter Everett, "The Beatles as Composers: The Genesis of *Abbey Road*, Side Two", in: Elizabeth West Marvin and Richard Hermann (eds.), *Concert Music, Rock, and Jazz since 1945: Essays and Analytical Studies*. Rochester, NY 1995, pp. 172–228; Everett has a monograph forthcoming. It is worth observing that his work falls into a tradition of critical assimilation of the Beatles that goes back to Wilfred Mellers and is proclaimed in the very title of his book *The Music of the Beatles: Twilight of the Gods*. New York 1973.

theoretical discourse, and an outstanding example of this is the work of Dave Headlam on Led Zeppelin.[39]

It is of course a fact of life that practically all rock music exists in multiple versions, including re-releases, remixes, covers, and any number of legitimate or bootlegged concert recordings, not to mention videos, films, and published transcriptions. (Where this is not the case, as for instance in the case of the music of Van Halen, it is likely to be the result of a carefully controlled policy of dissemination imposed by the artist or artists concerned.) But established theoretical approaches to music, derived as they are from the study of scores, are not well adapted to dealing with multiple versions.[40] Headlam recognizes that there is an issue here, but he sidesteps rather than confronts it: "One objection to my analytical treatment of the songs", he says, "might be that Led Zeppelin continually changed and evolved in their concert versions of these songs. For instance, concert versions of 'Dazed and Confused' ran to 45 minutes (...). Despite these improvisations, however, each song has a fixed studio version that has become definitive, and formed at least the basis for improvisations on stage. I consider the studio versions justification for my analysis."[41] In other words, he accepts the original releases as authoritative and simply discounts the other versions. The problem goes away.

It would be easy to condemn Headlam for ignoring the normal conditions of rock music and assimilating to the conditions of classical music, but this would be less than fair since precisely the same objection can be made in relation to the classical tradition. The writings of Lydia Goehr have accustomed us to the idea that the musical work is a historical construct dating from the years

---

39. Dave Headlam, "Does the Song Remain the Same? Questions of Authorship and identification in the Music of Led Zeppelin", in: Marvin and Hermann (eds.), *Concert Music, Rock, and Jazz since 1945*, pp. 313-363. I have discussed Everett's and Headlam's work briefly in my own contribution to Marvin and Hermann's volume ("Music Theory and the Postmodern Muse: An Afterword", pp. 422-439) and at greater length in "Music Minus One: Rock, Theory, and Performance", in: *New Formations* 27 (1995-1996), pp. 23-41.
40. For an extended discussion, see Nicholas Cook, "At the Borders of Musical Identity: Schenker, Corelli, and the Graces", in: *Music Analysis* 18, forthcoming.
41. Headlam, "Does the Song Remain the Same?", p. 332 n. 68.

around 1800, so that the concept of the single and definitive text was foreign to earlier periods (though there appears to be an emerging consensus that her second point is overstated).[42] In effect, Goehr is saying that nineteenth-century composers claimed for their music the qualities of uniqueness, authenticity, and unchangeability associated with the fine arts; hence the conceit of the 'imaginary museum' which gives her book its title. But if this is true for some composers (the paradigm case is Beethoven, the first composer to try and interest publishers in an authoritative edition of his complete works), for others it is simply not: for Chopin, for example, or Liszt, both of whose works often exist in a considerable number of versions, without there being any clear criteria according to which it might be asserted that one version is definitive while others are not.[43] And that is before one begins to consider the significance of the multiple versions in which *all* nineteenth-century music exists, that is to say, different performances. The wonder, then, is not that Headlam tries to fit Led Zeppelin into the Procrustean framework of the single and definitive version, but rather that the framework was ever considered an adequate basis for understanding *any* music.

Much the same can be said about the concept of undivided authorship. Here Headlam's problem is even more obvious: just who *is* the author of, say, Led Zeppelin's "Whole lotta love"? It does not suffice to regard the songwriter as the author (as Everett does in the case of the Beatles, where there is at least the justification of the generally distinctive quality of songs written by McCartney, Lennon, and Harrison), because "Whole lotta love" is adapted from the Chicago bluesman Willie Dixon's "You need love" — and a close enough adaptation, at that, for Dixon to have successfully sued Led Zeppelin on grounds of copyright

---

42. Lydia Goehr, *The Imaginary Museum of Musical Works: An Essay in the Philosophy of Music*. Oxford: Clarendon Press 1992. On music pre-1800 see Harry White, "'If It's Baroque, Don't Fix It': Reflections on Lydia Goehr's 'Work-Concept' and the Historical Integrity of Musical Composition", in: *Acta Musicologica* 59 (1997), pp. 94–104.
43. See Jeffrey Kallberg, *Chopin at the Boundaries: Sex, History, and Musical Genre*. Cambridge, Mass. 1996, chapter 7.

infringement.[44] If, following traditional musicological models, we were to regard Dixon as the author, that would reduce Led Zeppelin to the status of performers, whereas Headlam's whole aim is to establish the place of bands like Led Zeppelin within the composer-based canon of Western music. (Hence the prevalence in his article of value-laden terms such as the 'genuinely creative' reworking as against the 'merely derivative' cover — "Whole lotta love", of course, being an example of the former.[45]) So he resorts instead to a stratagem that not only constructs Led Zeppelin's status as authors, but in so doing assigns to the music theorist the role of arbiter that I discussed in the previous section.

Headlam shows how songs like "Whole Lotta Love", as he puts it, "share musical elements with the original versions, but are transformed formally, timbrally, rhythmically, motivically, and harmonically into the defining features of the Led Zeppelin sound".[46] In other words, Led Zeppelin integrate elements from Dixon's originals within a new synthesis, in rather the same way as Bach appropriated materials from Vivaldi. Headlam sees "Whole lotta love" as a reworking and not a cover because it has its own structural coherence: "The power and effect of 'Whole Lotta Love'", he says, "derives in large part from the formal contrast and combination of the two seemingly disparate elements — driving, rhythmic blues-riffs and free-form psychedelic effects — into a coherent whole".[47] And it is in this distinctive synthesis, in the unified 'sound' that characterizes the band as a whole, that Headlam locates Led Zeppelin's status as authors. But by now the idea of authorship has been transformed from its literal sense (in which it applies to one flesh-and-blood individual or another) to a new, theoretically-constructed sense, which Headlam explains by reference to Michel Foucault: "In this view," he says, "the 'author'

---

44. Headlam, "Does the Song Remain the Same?", p. 332, citing Willie Dixon with Don Snowden, *I am the Blues*. London 1989, pp. 217, 223.
45 Headlam's distinction between reworkings and covers, borrowed from Arnold Shaw, is closely parallel to the equally value-laden distinction between paraphrases and transcriptions made by Liszt's biographer, Alan Walker (*Franz Liszt: The Virtuoso Years 1811-1847*. London 1983, p. 167).
46. Headlam, "Does the Song Remain the Same?", p. 362.
47. Ibidem, p. 341.

constitutes a principle of unity among a class of works, somewhat akin to a theory, under which disparate works can be grouped together by their shared characteristics stemming from that authorship".[48] In this strange blend of post-structuralist theory and very traditional musical analysis, authorial status is not only demonstrable by the music theorist but paradigmatically undivided; after all, it is musical unity, the very stuff of analysis, that underwrites it.

It seems that Headlam is himself less than fully convinced by this convoluted argument, for throughout his article he remains undecided as to whether Led Zeppelin should take a single or a plural verb. And the most revealing thing about the argument is precisely its convoluted nature, which reveals the depth of Headlam's investment (and, by extension, that of music theory in general) in the concept of undivided authorship. For the multiple authorship that characterizes popular music production goes a great deal further than the collectivity of band composition; it extends to the highly segmented processes in which the roles of song-writers, arrangers, and artists are complemented by those of sound engineers, producers, and A&R personnel. Not infrequently several of these roles are combined in a single individual, but the roles themselves are largely distinct and increasingly credited as such on CDs; even samples may be individually credited. And whereas such credits are in part a response to the actual or perceived demands of copyright legislation, they also reflect an aesthetic valuation, in line with the creative influence that popular music historians have long ascribed to, say, Phil Spector. Multiple authorship, in short, is not only a fact of life but an interpretive principle in popular music.

Lisa Lewis has commented of the current system of assigning credit that it "represents only a small modification in the model of individual authorship in that it maintains the focus on the individual rather than the collective. Because no consensus for collective authorship has emerged to counter the historical focus on the individual author (despite the collectivity of modern production),

---

48. Ibidem, p. 327.

authorship discourse has become increasingly conflicted and contradictory under industrial capitalism."[49] And she adds that a symptom of this conflicted nature may be seen in the mismatch between the actuality of popular music production and the perception of fans who, in contradistinction to popular music historians, "often assume that the performer is also the composer". But such mismatches are by no means restricted to popular music. Lydia Goehr, citing Daniel Barenboim and Theodor Adorno, suggests that audiences sometimes think of classical conductors as themselves playing or even composing the music.[50] By contrast, histories of classical music (especially popular histories) tend to emphasize the role of composers at the almost total expense of other participants in the creative process; they call themselves histories of music but are really histories of compositions. It would be hard, however, to argue that the production of music in the eighteenth or nineteenth centuries was significantly less segmented than that of popular music today. If there is an essential difference, it is that the different creative roles are predominantly simultaneous in popular music (which makes them harder to distinguish from one another), whereas in classical music they tend to be sequential. Paradoxically, then, you might claim that authorship is not less but more obviously divided in classical than in popular music.

If such a claim appears tendentious, the reason lies less in the facts of the matter than in the ideological baggage wrapped up with the concept of authorship. It is easy enough to instance cases in which music received as the work of one composer is in fact the product of a collaboration, though generally at a temporal remove: Mozart/Süssmayr, Mussorgsky/Rimsky-Korsakov, and so forth. (If these names evoke painful critical controversies, that is only

---

49. Lisa A. Lewis, *Gender Politics and MTV: Voicing the Difference*. Philadelphia 1990, pp. 64–65.
50. Goehr, *The Imaginary Museum*, p. 276. Schoenberg thought along similar lines when he compained that "Today [performers] stand higher than creators; they were put there not by themselves but by the favor of a public that believes that music comes from reproducers, just as miracles were attributed to the priest, not to God", in: Arnold Schoenberg (Patricia Carpenter and Severine Neff, ed.), *The Musical Idea and the Logic, Technique, and Art of its Presentation*. New York 1995, pp. 291–293.

evidence of the ideological baggage to which I referred.) And until a generation ago it was quite normal to perform the classical repertory in versions adapted to the modern pianoforte or symphony orchestra, giving rise to Bach/Busoni, [C.P.E.] Bach/Bülow or Beethoven/Weingartner, for example. (As I have elsewhere written, "The idea of the *Urtext*, like that of historical performance practice, goes back to the days of Brahms, but its acceptance as the norm of informed performance dates back hardly further than the 1960s. It is as if the tenets of modernism became established in performance only at the dawn of postmodernism.")[51] But these examples, together with the overt practices of collaborative authorship characteristic of the opera, pale into insignificance beside the creative collaboration as which performance must be seen, as soon as we acknowledge its significance as a locus of aesthetic effect. Just as in the case of multiple versions (and it is of course here that multiple versions and multiple authorship fuse into a single concept), what is striking is less the phenomenon than the way in which we swerve away from it.

So what is the ideological baggage to which I have referred? To say that as established religion declined its place was taken by art (and in particular music) may be a cliché, but it is also a fact. Again it is Goehr who documents the attribution of divine characteristics to composers by nineteenth-century commentators, revealing a nice hierarchy that begins with Baini's 1828 description of Palestrina as an early 'amanuensis of God', passes through Samuel Wesley's various characterizations of [J.S.] Bach as a 'Saint', a 'Musical High Priest', and a 'Demi-God', and concludes predictably enough with Bizet's description of Beethoven as a God.[52] But it is Schenker, writing in the 1920s, who provides perhaps the most unequivocal testament to the true source of musical creativity when he writes that true coherence — the coherence to which his theory alone gives access — is found only in "God and (...) the geniuses through whom he works".[53] And Peter Kivy

---

51. Cook, "Music Minus One", p. 32.
52. Goehr, *The Imaginary Museum*, p. 208.
53. Heinrich Schenker (Ernst Oster, ed. and transl.), *Free Composition (Der freie Satz)*. New York 1979, pp. i, 160.

has emphasized the extent to which concepts of musical creation current throughout the nineteenth century and into Schenker's time drew on theological models. The principal witness for his case is the famous letter attributed to Mozart but almost certainly fabricated by Friedrich Rochlitz in 1815, which speaks of the composer hearing all the parts of his music in his imagination not in succession but "as it were, all at once";[54] Kivy shows through quotation from Boethius and Aquinas that Rochlitz was simply rewriting a standard theological chestnut ("How does God, who is eternal and unchanging, conceive of the course of history?")[55] in terms of music.

The fact that Mozart never wrote the words that were attributed to him does not detract from their significance as a reflection and indeed a shaping agent in nineteenth- and early twentieth-century thinking on the subject, for the spurious letter was widely quoted (including by Schenker).[56] Indeed its reflections may be traced in certain twentieth-century views about performance, in particular Erwin Stein's statement of the performer's need to have the "whole piece in a nutshell in his mind".[57] The high profile which the letter came to occupy is hardly surprising in view of the way in which it brought together a number of highly resonant concepts: the divine nature of artistic creation, the authority inherent in the primordial vision of the work, and the actually or potentially demonstrable unity which underwrites the vision. It is the last two of these which have practical consequences for music and in particular for the conceptualization of performance. Just as the textual criticism practised by biblical and classical philologists

---

54. Peter Kivy, "Mozart and Monotheism", in: *The Fine Art of Repetition: Essays in the Philosophy of Music*. Cambridge 1993, pp. 189-199, especially p. 189. Kivy provides all necessary references, except that it might be added that Maynard Solomon's essay has been reprinted in his *Beethoven Essays*. Cambridge, Mass. 1988, pp. 126-138. For a further account of late Romantic parallels between divine and artistic creation, see Carl Dahlhaus, "Schoenberg's Aesthetic Ideology", in: Derrick Puffett and Alfred Clayton (transl.), *Schoenberg and the New Music: Essays by Carl Dahlhaus*. Cambridge 1987, pp. 81-93.
55. Kivy, "Mozart and Monotheism", p. 195.
56. Schenker, *Free Composition (Der freie Satz)*, pp. i, 129.
57. Erwin Stein, *Form and Performance*. London 1962, p. 71.

sought to strip off the accretions of time and reconstruct the original version of the text, so the musical *Urtext* strives to recapture the composer's original vision; hence the endurance, long after its abandonment in other disciplines, of a language of intentionality originally associated with 'authentic' editions but subsequently transferred to 'authentic' performances. Authority, in short, is seen to derive from the composer, being delegated (but only delegated) to the editors of 'authoritative' editions and to the conductors or other charismatic performers who stand in, so to speak, for the composer when the music is played.

This is of course the source of the unusually strict hierarchies that characterize the practice of music, as reflected for instance in Leonard Bernstein's not entirely convincing stipulation that the conductor "be humble before the composer; that he never interpose himself between the music and the audience; that all his efforts, however strenuous or glamorous, be made in the service of the composer's meaning — the music itself, which after all, is the whole reason for the conductor's existence".[58] Bernstein's invocation of 'the music itself' as the object of the composer's loyalty is a necessary reminder that the hierarchy of musical authority is not, in the first place, a hierarchy of individuals (composer, editor, conductor, rank-and-file player) but rather what might be termed a hierarchy of content. In calling it this I have in mind the text-oriented concept of music which Schenker evoked when he proclaimed in the preface of his monograph on the Ninth Symphony that "In the beginning was content [*Inhalt*]!", thereby aligning music with the divine Word of St John's Gospel;[59] the perhaps baleful influence that philology exerted over the early development of musicology is undoubtedly a major source of the difficulties we encounter in conceptualizing music as a performance art in the full sense of this term. But it is more particularly to the third concept embraced by Rochlitz's fabrication that I wish to refer, namely the unity that underlines the composer's vision.

---

58. Leonard Bernstein, *The Joy of Music*. London 1959, p. 56 (quoted in Goehr, *The Imaginary Museum*, p. 276).
59. Schenker, *Beethoven's Ninth Symphony*, p. 4.

As so often it is Schenker who, through the very extremity of his ideas, reveals what is at issue most vividly. When I spoke of the editor stripping of the accretions of time and reconstructing the original version of the text, I could easily have been quoting *verbatim* from Schenker. But Schenker distanced himself from the *Urtext* of his day, which he saw as representing the "letter-worship of antiquarian sticklers for literalness, whose adoration is sometimes extended to misprints".[60] While he shared the same goal as editors like Bischoff, he did not avail himself of their philologically-inspired methods. Instead he relied on analysis of content — analysis of the music itself, to repeat Bernstein's words. A representative example of his approach towards text criticism may be found in the 1925 essay on Chopin's Gb major Study, Op. 10 No. 5, where he discusses the issue of whether there should be a gb^3 or (as the autograph and most editions have it) an eb^3 in bar 24.[61]

As usual, Schenker begins by setting up a fall guy, in this case Hugo Leichtentritt, according to whom "It is almost impossible to point with certainty to any one reading rather than another as being the authentic one". At this point Schenker jumps in with an ironically self-effacing rejoinder: "If I may be so bold as to say so, authenticity [i.e. traditional text-critical method] does not dictate

---

60. Preface to C.P.E. Bach (Heinrich Schenker, ed.), *Klavierwerke*. Vienna 1902.
61. Schenker, "Chopin: Etude in Gb major, Op. 10, No. 5", in: William Drabkin (ed.), *The Masterwork in Music: A Yearbook. Volume 1 (1925)*. Cambridge 1994, pp. 90–98, especially p. 98; for further discussion of this example (and more generally of Schenker's editorial work) see Nicholas Cook, "The Editor and the virtuoso, or Schenker versus Bülow", in: *Journal of the Royal Musical Association* 116 (1991), pp. 78–95. Schenker's editorial practice represents only an extreme case of the application of a principle of unity that is widespread in the *Urtext*, namely the assimilation of multiply appearing material to a single format assumed to be authoritative. What is at issue is not so much the often arbitrary criteria by which such authoritativeness is judged, but rather the assumption that composers intended near-literal repeats to be identical, or different parts within a homophonic texture to be articulated in precisely the same manner, even though this is not what they actually wrote. For the argument that such small discrepancies were intended, and that the standardization adopted by most editors represents the imposition of an extraneous aesthetic ideology, see Graham Pont, "A Revolution in the Science and Practice of Music", in: *Musicology* [=*Musicology Australia*] 5 (1979), pp. 1–66 and Dene Barnett, "Non-uniform Slurring in 18th Century Music: Accident or Design?", in: *Haydn Yearbook* 10 (1977), pp. 179–199.

on matters of voice-leading." For him the matter is settled by analytical demonstration (as shown in his Figure 1, the middleground ab^3 of bar 21 falls to gb^3 in bar 23 and remains active until bar 41); Chopin simply wrote down the wrong note. And now Schenker presses home his advantage: "it is inexcusable to grant a slip of the pen that produces eb^3 on one occasion instead of gb^3 the status of an authentic reading. These matters are far simpler than people think: voice-leading is a higher entity than Chopin; had it not governed him, we would have not a single master-stroke by him! How extraordinary, and how utterly typical of man, that he so often takes the genius's slip of the pen at face value and invests it with canonical status; and, still more often, he has no scruples about taking something that is perfectly correct and imputing an error to the genius, labelling it a 'reading'. Quite extraordinary!"

When Schenker says that "voice-leading is a higher entity than Chopin" he means it quite literally: there is an authority higher than that of the composer, even the genius-composer, and it is to this higher authority that appeal is to be made when the composer does the wrong thing. On another occasion Schenker explains how, in composing the "Heiliger Dankgesang" of the String Quartet in A Minor, Op. 132, Beethoven had the clear intention of writing in the Lydian mode, which (like all the church modes, as Schenker explains) represents merely a transitional and imperfect phase in the development of major-minor tonality. But as Oswald Jonas, Schenker's editor, glosses the text, even Beethoven could not write "in a 'Lydian system' which, in reality, never existed";[62] the composer, in short, was determined to do the wrong thing. And yet the music turns out to have a deep coherence that derives not from the so-called Lydian system but from the principles of major-minor tonality from which Beethoven thought he was getting away. How could this be? Beethoven had no idea, replies Schenker in a memorable image, that "behind his back there stood that higher force of Nature and led his pen, forcing his composition into F major while he himself was sure he was composing in

---

62. Heinrich Schenker (Oswald Jonas, ed., Elisabeth Mann Borgese, transl.), *Harmony*. Chicago 1954, p. 61 n. 3.

the Lydian mode, merly because that was his conscious will and intention. Is that not marvellous? And yet it is so."[63]

Whether one personifies this higher authority as God or Nature, or characterizes it more prosaically in terms of physical, psychological, or even historical laws, makes little difference in the end: the composer speaks, but with a voice that is not, in the limiting case, his or her own. And here Schenker finds himself in an unlikely alliance with intellectual traditions ranging from Freudian psychoanalysis to French poststructuralism, each of which invokes an explanatory domain removed from individual consciousness. Like Barthes, Schenker proclaims the death of the Author[64] (and the intersection of Schenker and Barthes provides the model for the hardly more probable linkage of Headlam and Foucault). But there is a significant difference, for the beneficiary is not in Schenker's case the reader but the theorist, who alone has intellectual access to the truth. Again the model can be interpreted as in essence a theological one: if in Schenker's system the genius-composers resemble mystics in their direct intuition of a higher plane, the theorist assumes the role of the ecclesiastical authorities, translating higher truths into terms accessible to ordinary people and thereby exercising a mediating function.[65] (The fact that, in case of difference, it is the latter who have jurisdiction over the former only strengthens the parallel; in religion as in music, the Word may emanate from God but it is subject to interpretation at a more local level.)

There is, then, a hierarchy of authority in music but, as Schenker presents it, it is a hierarchy grounded in musical content and its correct interpretation. And while Schenker's characteristically fundamentalist blend of extremism and literal-mindedness gives a picturesque quality to his presentation, it embodies (only in more concentrated form) patterns of thought so widespread that we

---

63. Ibidem, pp. 60–61.
64. Roland Barthes, "The Death of the Author", in: Barthes (Stephen Heath, transl.), *Image Music Text*. London 1977, pp. 142–148.
65. Through "the being who is stronger than they", writes Schenker, the masses "can vicariously entertain elevating thoughts about religion, art, or science; but these heady thoughts are soon gone, and the masses are back where they were" (*The Masterwork in Music, Volume I*, p. 115).

generally fail to recognize them as such. We may not be able to accept Schenker's notion of genius-composers or the priest-like role that he assigns to the theorist except by virtue of an effort of historical understanding, but the great chain of being that he outlines between God and the ordinary person is replicated in the hierarchical structures of contemporary music theory.[66] (If the bottom level of a prolongational hierarchy, say, represents the moment-to-moment perceptions of a listener, the topmost nodes have no correlate in perceptual experience and so correspond to what might be termed the 'God's-eye view' embraced by Rochlitz's account of the composer's vision.) And we commonly think of performers as exercising the same priest-like function, that is to say as occupying a position intermediate between creation and reception. In short (and here at last I come to the third musicological concept to which I referred at the beginning of this section), we think of composer, performer, and listener as occupying successive points within a single, linear structure.

Although it is with this linear structure that I shall finally be concerned, it is worth exploring the affinities between priest and performer a little further. In Bernstein's imprecation that all the conductor's efforts, "however strenuous or glamorous, be made in the service of the composer's meaning", even the subjunctive mode contributes to the religious connotation; it is as if Bernstein were putting himself forward as the Billy Graham of music. And the conspicuous tension in the evangelical community between service on the one hand and glamour on the other, between God and Mammon, also translates to the world of conducting. On the one hand, in his or her interpretive role the conductor is the most visible link in the musical chain; hence Schoenberg's sour reference, which I have already quoted,[67] to "the public that believes that music comes from reproducers, just as miracles were attributed to the priest, not to God". But on the other hand the conductor, like

---

66. For a discussion of the affinities between traditional conceptions of the great chain of being and music theory see Lawrence Zbikowski, "Conceptual Models and Cross-Domain Mapping: New Perspectives on Theories of Music and Hierarchy", in: *Journal of Music Theory* 41 (1997), pp. 193–225.

67. See above, n. 50.

all mediators, is supposed to aim at self-effacement; Liszt wrote that "the genuine task of a conductor consists in making himself, manifestly superfluous",[68] and so we are once again back at the ideal of transparency that we have already encountered in relation to Bülow and Brahms. Indeed I have already quoted the most uncompromising statement of this position, namely Schoenberg's assertion that the performer is "totally unnecessary except as his interpretations make the music understandable to an audience unfortunate enough not to be able to read it in print".

It would be silly to equate a statement like this, presumably made off the cuff, with a considered theoretical stance. But it is precisely unconsidered statements that reveal deeply embedded premises most clearly, and the same applies to Schoenberg's even more reckless confession of "dreams of a possibility of expression (...) where one may speak with kindred spirits in the language of intuition and know that one is understood if one uses the speech of the imagination — of fantasy".[69] Whereas in the first of these statements the performer represents an essentially redundant halfway house between score and audience, in the second the score itself becomes transparent: music speaks from mind to mind through some esoteric telepathy, eliminating all mediation. And once again there is a widespread, if on the whole less extravagantly expressed, assumption that scores are merely an intermediate stage in a linear conveyance of content from composer to listener. The demonstration that scores are not just intermediate points in a linear process of communication is easiest in the case of contemporary music. After all, graphic scores like John Cage's *Solo for Piano* or Cornelius Cardew's *Treatise* are essentially indeterminate with respect to their acoustic realization, and therefore if they are to be regarded as conveying anything from composer to listener that something must be of a highly abstract or generic nature.[70] Or

---

68. Franz Liszt, "A Letter on Conducting" (1853), quoted by Lydia Goehr in: *The Imaginary Museum*, p. 276.
69. Arnold Schoenberg (Leonard Stein, ed.), *Style and Idea*. Berkeley 1984, pp. 274-275.
70. Both examples and argument are taken from Tom Service, "Representations: Contemporary Music and the Myth of Unmediated Transparency". MA diss., University of Southampton 1998, pp. 4-11.

to take another example, Berio's *Gesti* for alto recorder involves a special notation which separates the two principal sites of activity in playing the instrument: the mouth and the fingers.[71] The mouth part, if it can be called that, is notated with a high degree of specificity (fluttertongue, lip tension, singing through the instrument, inhaling) but the part for the fingers simply calls for repeated playing of one or two bars (any one or two bars) from a particular Telemann sonata. The juxtaposition of the two parts is indeterminate and therefore, as Berio states in the score, "the resulting sound is unpredictable. (…) Sometimes the instrument will produce no sound at all." The effect of the music in performance is attributable less to specific coincidences between notation and sonic outcome than to the way in which it deconstructs and reconstructs the player's technique. In conventional recorder performance, hands and lip are coordinated around the music that is to be played. But Berio's fragmented notation dislocates this coordination, creating an effect that is not so much represented as constructed by the score. To put it another way, the score functions performatively, as a site for the emergence of new sounds and new signification.

Nor need such demonstrations be limited to examples of compositional indeterminacy. Much the same points might be made about music which is, so to speak, overdetermined with respect to its performance. I have in mind music such as Stockhausen's *Klavierstück I*, the aggressively complex notation of which is surely to be understood less as the representation of specifically envisaged acoustic effects than as a statement which was on the one hand ideological and on the other hand performative: with its multi-level, irrational rhythms, huge leaps and disdain of familiar pianistic patterns, *Klavierstück I* defied literal rendition and so demanded a reconstruction of technique in very much the same way as *Gesti*. Of course there is a problem with this kind of compositional overdetermination, which is that last year's Parnassus becomes next year's examination piece, and the work of certain 'New Complexity' composers (Brian Ferneyhough is a

---

71. This account of *Gesti* is condensed from Cook, "Music Minus One", p. 37.

conspicuous example) can be seen as an attempt to update the kind of performative encounter that *Klavierstück I* embodied in 1953.[72] Such encounters force a reflective distance upon the performer by shattering the apparent transparency of the score as a representation of acoustic intention. Under such circumstances the familiar, if untheorized, identification of work and score becomes plainly inadequate, and Ferneyhough reflects this when he speaks of the "realm of non-equivalence" between score and performance being "where, perhaps, the 'work' might be said to be ultimately located".[73] And Lawrence Rosenwald has made the very similar suggestion that a musical piece should be understood as "something existing in the relation between the notation and the field of its performances".[74] Seen this way, score and performance are simulacra neither of one another, nor of "the piece itself, whatever that phrase might mean", as Rosenwald puts it. It is instead the difference between the various representations that counts.

At this point I anticipate an objection: "You have shown the lack of transparency between work, score, and sound in the avant-garde repertory. But that repertory is defined just by its oppositional relation to conventional music styles, in which transparency is accordingly the norm." As it happens, however, Rosenwald is not talking about the avant-garde repertory at all. He is talking about Beethoven's Ninth Symphony, about the way in which 'the piece' (in any aesthetically useful sense of the term) has steadily acquired new signification since its completion in 1824, as a result of successive critical and performance interpretations. When we hear the Ninth Symphony, we hear it against a horizon of expectations established by past performances and especially by recordings: a new interpretation signifies by virtue not only of what it is, but also of the pattern of differences it establishes with respect to the interpretations of Mengelberg, Toscanini, Furtwängler,

---

72. See in this context Service's discussion of Ferneyhough's *Trittico per G.S.* for solo double bass, in: "Representations", pp. 19–21.
73. James Boros and Richard Toop (eds.), *Collected Writings of Brian Ferneyhough.* Amsterdam 1995, p. 13 (quoted and discussed in Service, "Representations", p. 21).
74. Lawrence Rosenwald, "Theory, Text-setting, and Performance", in: *Journal of Musicology* 11 (1993), pp. 52–65, especially p. 62.

Karajan, Norrington, Hogwood, Harnoncourt. In acknowledging the co-relativity of score and performance, Rosenwald's formulation asserts that neither can be adequately understood as an ideally transparent representation of a predefined content. Instead, both score and performance are to be understood performatively, as sites for the construction rather than merely the reproduction of meaning. And they operate through a process of dialectic engagement, with performances being interpreted in light of the score, and the score being interpreted in light of performances.

What this amounts to is taking seriously Rothstein's idea, which I have already quoted, that "the performer adopts temporarily the viewpoint of one or two characters in the drama, so to speak, rather than assuming omniscience at every moment." For the deeply-embedded assumptions about performance whose archaeology I have traced might be described as converging precisely on the idea of omniscience. The authoritative understanding nominally possessed by the God-like composer (but actually exercised, in case of dispute, by the theorist) is delegated in the manner of a management hierarchy to the performer, who is expected to convey the same authoritative understanding to the listener; this is the context for the hierachical relationship between theorist and performer that I traced in the previous section. Rothstein means that the performer should indeed have this knowledge, but should sometimes pretend not to. In other words, like a novelist, he or she should sometimes present the story from a particular protagonist's view, while still of course controlling all the strings. But a more radical reading of Rothstein's formulation would question the very possibility (or desirability) of omniscience, and with it what Kevin Korsyn calls "a central point of intelligibility".[75]

In contrast to traditional music theory, Korsyn advocates an approach drawn from Bakhtin's theory of the novel, the premise of which is the multiplicity of linguistic levels which Bakhtin terms 'heteroglossia'. For Bakhtin, the meaning of a novel arises from the irreducible heterogeneity of its linguistic constituents,

---

75. Kevin Korsyn, "Beyond Privileged Contexts: Intertextuality, Influence, and Dialogue", in: Cook and Everist (eds.), *Rethinking Music*, pp. 55–72, especially p. 65.

and is in this sense emergent. And he characterizes the unity of a novel as dialogic rather than dialectic, the difference being that the dialectic resolves opposition into a higher unity whereas, in Paul de Man's words, "the function of dialogism is to sustain and think through the radical exteriority or heterogeneity of one voice with regard to any other, including that of the novelist himself."[76] (From a Bakhtinian viewpoint, then, I should have said 'dialogic' rather than 'dialectic' in the paragraph before last.) Transform 'novelist' into 'composer' and you have a formulation that applies as well to musical performance as it does does to the novel. For performance embodies in the most literal manner the interaction of multiple agencies. Seen this way, the idea of a linear relationship or great chain of being in which score and performance occupy intermediate positions is replaced by a multi-dimensional structure that incorporates, minimally, the score, the performance, and an interpreter (who will always be a listener and may or may not also be the performer). And even that is an idealization, for a more comprehensive model would also include the multiple agencies of ensemble performance, the composer (now understood as a critical construction rather than a historical agent), and the horizon of expectations constituted, as I said, by performance as well as critical interpretations.

In emphasizing the construction rather than the reproduction of meaning, a genuinely performative model of performance would distance itself not only from the idea of 'reproducing' the musical content (as in the quotations from Brahms and Schoenberg), but also from easy and prevailing ideas of the 'translation' of structure into performance. In his review of Berry's *Musical Structure and Performance* Rink complained with justification of "too simplistic a translation from analysis to performance".[77] And while Rink has himself continued to use the term (as in "Translating Musical Meaning"), it might be considered more prudent to avoid it alto-

---

76. Paul de Man, *The Resistance to Theory*. Minneapolis 1986, p. 109, quoted in Korsyn, "Beyond Privileged Contexts", p. 61.
77. John Rink, review of Wallace Berry, *Musical Structure and Performance,* in: *Music Analysis* 9 (1990), pp. 319–339, especially p. 321.

gether; after all, when we think of translation, we normally think of the substantive context that can be equally well expressed in French or German, say, rather than the more intangible connotations that defy translation. But it is once again Rosenwald who points out that there is also what might be termed a strong sense of translation which turns on the semantic friction between languages, and he adds that it is precisely through the attempt at translation, through straining at the limitations of any system of representation, that we gain an understanding of content: "we do not know the original", he says, "do not and cannot know it *in se*, and (...) come to know it precisely by means of reflecting on its translations."[78] And in his commentary on Rosenwald's article, Fred Maus adds that "in this process of exploration the distinction between 'making' and 'finding' meanings is obscure".[79]

Rosenwald and Maus are talking about analytical rather than performance interpretation, but the distinction that Maus makes is precisely the same as the one I have been making between the constructive and the reproductive aspects of performance. And in truth, a performative approach to analysis and a performative approach to performance will almost inevitably go hand in hand, for the one implies the other.[80]

IN PLACE OF CLOSURE

If it is true that, as Lester says, the study of actual performance is singularly absent from music-theoretical discourse, then this may be principally put down to the entrenched ways of thought that I discussed in the previous section. But it may also be put down to something more straightforward and practical. Modern music theory (in contradistinction to pre-modern speculative traditions) is built upon empirical resistance. The interface between word and

---

78. Rosenwald, "Theory, Text-setting, and Performance", p. 62.
79. Fred Maus, "Response to Rosenwald", in: *Journal of Musicology* 11 (1993), pp. 66–72, especially p. 69.
80. For further discussion of analytical performativity see Cook, "Analysing Performance, and Performing Analysis", from which the present argument is condensed.

music in theoretical discourse has evolved since the mid-nineteenth century from a purely ostensive one (with music examples, if present at all, being limited to score extracts) to increasingly focussed analysis, with the music being graphically dissected and reconstructed in tandem with the verbal text. In other words, a genre of writing has been established which embodies a relatively stable (if rarely theorized) blend of empirical data, logical demonstration, and rhetoric.[81] But there is as yet no established genre for theoretical writing about performance; we have little idea of what epistemological blend we should be aiming at.[82] And until recently there were no commonly-accepted techniques providing the same kind of empirical grasp on performance that we take for granted when writing about scores. The danger, then, was one of relapsing when writing onto performance into the kind of subjective and impressionistic writing that professionalized music theory had left behind. As a result, and despite the accumulation of a repertory of recordings that now goes back a century, performance analysis remains in a state of academic infancy.

Within the past decade the situation has changed to the extent that there is now a variety of tools for capturing different aspects of recorded sound and translating them (if that is the right word) into a graphic or numerical format. The cleanest data is obtained from MIDI instruments, which in the case of the MIDI-equipped piano enables a concise and comprehensive representation of the different dimensions of performance variance. But such data are, of course, unavailable for the historical repertory of recordings, for which recourse must be made to some kind of acoustically-based analysis. Some techniques, which currently occupy the status of curiosities rather than accepted methods, are at a high level of

---

81. For an attempt to theorize this blend, with references, see Nicholas Cook, "Epistemologies of Music Theory", in: Thomas Christensen (ed.), *The Cambridge History of Music Theory*. Cambridge forthcoming.
82. I would also suggest that the process of generic condensation in theoretical writing involved the development of appropriate aural training practices (that is, enabling the linking of graphic representation and experienced effect), and that the need for corresponding skills is another impediment to the rapid development of performance analysis. (For example, you cannot just look at Figure 1 below and know how it will translate into experienced sound, but you can *learn* to make the link.)

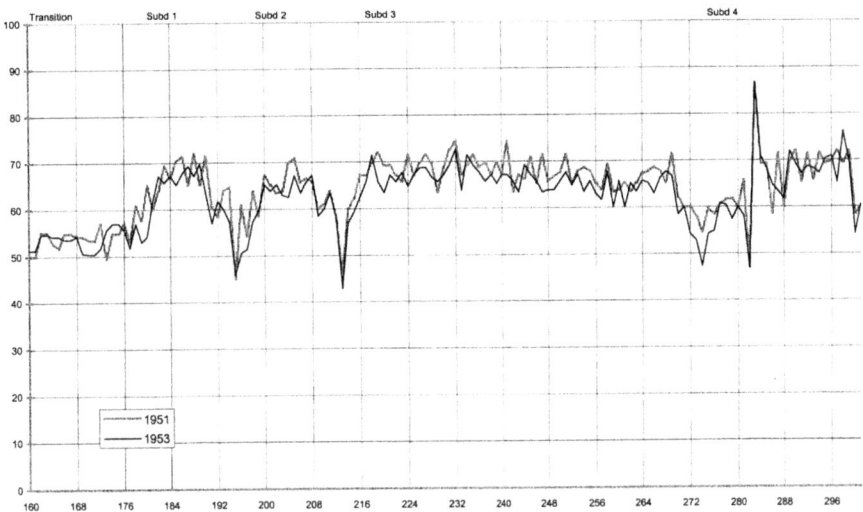

Figure 1

abstraction (for instance Neil Todd's 'rhythmograms')[83] or provide highly summarized synopses of musical structure (Robert Cogan's spectrographic analyses).[84] Others operate at a lower level and of these the most frequently used by far is duration analysis. In the commonest variant of this technique, the analyst listens to the recording and at certain points depresses a key on a computer, which logs the time at which the key is depressed. These points might be irregularly placed structural divisions, or they might be the beginning of every bar or half-bar; in the latter case, analysis of the logged times will result in a series of tempo values which may be plotted against time. Figure 1 is an example of such a

---

83. Neil Todd, "The Auditory 'Primal Sketch': A Multiscale Model of Rhythmic Grouping", in: *Journal of New Music Research* 23 (1994), pp. 25–70, summarized in Eric Clarke, "Expression in Performance: Generativity, Perception and Semiosis", in: Rink, *The Practice of Performance*, pp. 21–54, especially p. 24. Todd's rhythmograms consist of intensity information passed through a series of filters operating on different time scales.

84. Robert Cogan, *New Images of Musical Sound*. Cambridge, Mass. 1984. Peter Johnson has applied spectrographic analysis at a much more detailed level; his work, currently unpublished, was briefly outlined during the 1998 Seminar of the Orpheus Institute.

graph, representing the first movement development section from Beethoven's Ninth Symphony as performed by Furtwängler on two separate live recordings, dating from 1951 and 1953.[85]

I have already referred to Furtwängler's enthusiastic response to Schenker's monograph on the Ninth Symphony, as a result of which he not only established a personal relationship with Schenker but routinely discussed with him the music that he was preparing for performance.[86] It stands to reason, then, that there should be some kind of affinity between Schenker's analytical approach to the Ninth Symphony and Furtwängler's manner of performing it (and reciprocally that Furtwängler's recordings, though dating from more than fifteen years after Schenker's death, should provide some insight into the kind of performance that Schenker had in mind). And indeed this proves to be the case. In his monograph, Schenker offers a segmentation of the development section (he sees bars 160-179 as a transitional passage followed by four distinct subdivisions at bars 180-197, 198-217, 218-274, and 275-300), and claims that "the performance of the Development will be the better the more its subdivisions (...) are given clear expression as such".[87] This segmentation is easily detectable in the tempo graph of Furtwängler's performances, with the first two subdivisions outlined by a pattern of increasing and decreasing tempi (giving rise to arch-shaped profiles), the

---

85. Figure 5.2 from Nicholas Cook, "The Conductor and the Theorist", in: Rink, *The Practice of Performance*, pp. 105-125, where further discussion of this tempo-mapping technique may be found, and from which the following paragraphs are condensed. (The recordings are respectively available on EMI CDH 7 69801 2 and DG 435 325-2.) For a concise introduction to a range of tempo-mapping applications see José Antonio Bowen, "Tempo, Duration, and Flexibility: Techniques in the Analysis of Performance", in: *Journal of Musicological Research* 16 (1996), pp. 111-156. Mention should also be made of Robert Philip's *Early Recordings and Musical Style: Changing Tastes in Instrumental Performance, 1900-1950*. Cambridge 1992; this is a landmark work in terms of bringing recorded performances within the musicological purview, but limited in its approach to empirical analysis.
86. For details of the Schenker-Furtwängler relationship see Hellmut Federhofer, *Heinrich Schenker Nach Tagebüchern und Briefen in der Oswald Jonas Memorial Collection*. Hildesheim 1985, pp. 106-133. In 1954 Furtwängler published a short article on Schenker (translated as "Heinrich Schenker: A Contemporary Problem", in: *Sonus* 6 (1985), pp. 1-5).
87. Schenker, *Beethoven's Ninth Symphony*, p. 97.

third by a passage of relatively stable tempo, and the last by a less clear profile which might be described as an overall accelerando divided at bars 282–283 by a kind of agogic accent.[88] (The lack of clarity at this point might be put down to the way in which the music wears its structure, so to speak, on its sleeve, thus mandating a relatively neutral interpretation on the conductor's part.) But within these subdivisions Schenker constantly gives the impression of asking for two contradictory things.

On the one hand, in accordance with the demands of articulate performance, Schenker specifies numerous small nuances, which Furtwängler (like other conductors of his day) duly provides. But on the other, Schenker repeatedly insists on the need to create a sense of large-scale movement across each subdivision; one must summon all one's powers, he says, "to direct one's consciousness immediately, exactly upon entering the first subdivision — thus as early as bars 180–181! —, toward the cadence of bar 192ff, which awaits beyond the 'mountain pass' of bars 188–194; that is, one must organize the performance of the subdivision according to a kind of bird's-eye view, a premonition of the overall course of the subdivision from its first tonic up to the last cadence. Only then will the cadence be performed as a cadence to the whole subdivision and not, as we unfortunately hear all too often, as a new unit in itself."[89]

The sort of bitty effect that Schenker is disparaging can be heard on the recording that Mengelberg made with the Concertgebouw Orchestra in 1940; instead of integrating bars 192–197 within the subdivision of which it forms the cadence, Mengelberg drops speed substantially at bar 192, so giving this point as much weight as bar 197. Furtwängler, by contrast, nuances bar 192 (in each of his recordings there is a point of reversal at bar 192) but subordinates it to the main cadence.

---

88. Properly speaking (i.e. as defined by Hugo Riemann), an agagogic accent is a structural note emphasized by lengthening (see Philip, *Early Recordings*, pp. 41–42). I am broadening the term to include the emphasis that results from a rallentando or caesura prior to the note in question, i.e. to designate all emphases resulting from rubato.
89. Ibidem. What Schenker terms a 'bird's-eye view' corresponds, of course, to what I previously referred to as a 'God's-eye view'.

Now it is a generally accepted, though more rarely theorized, principle of performance that agogic accents serve to articulate points of structural division, with the intensity of the accent corresponding to structural embedding depth; in other words, a small agogic accent will correspond to a minor structural division, and a larger accent to a major division. But this principle, based on the assumption of a generally static tempo, establishes merely a linear continuum from minor to major division. Furtwängler's arch-shaped tempo profiles, by contrast, establish a qualitative distinction between what might be termed the structural and the rhetorical: on the one hand, the structural reversal which splits off one arch-shaped profile from another, and on the other the local nuance which, as at bar 192, is embraced within the larger profile. Furtwängler, in short, not only provides a correlate in performance of Schenker's structural spans, but finds an equivalent in performance for the multi-level structure of Schenker's theory (in which a foreground event might be described as 'rhetorical' with respect to a middleground, or 'structural', one). And the result is that Furtwängler is able to synthesize what in Schenker's account look like contradictory demands into a single, compelling interpretation. In short, Furtwängler's performance realizes a meaning that Schenker's words can only hint at.

But how adequate is this as a model for the analysis of performance? We can dispose relatively quickly of some general complaints that have been raised against the analysis of recordings. One complaint is that they are unreliable, in the sense that you cannot tell how far the audible balance is an artefact of the recording process (the position of performers in relation to the horn in an early recording, microphone placement in a more recent one), or how far tone colour has been distorted by technology. Or again, given the variability in speed of early recording apparatus, you cannot tell whether the music you are hearing was performed in one tempo at A=440 or in a slower tempo at A=420. But information does not need to be perfectly reliable in order for you to analyze it; we routinely talk about the effect of early music on the basis of scores, when in reality we have far less idea how it sounded than the music on the records. (And the problem about recording speeds only affects absolute, not relative, tempi.) A similar but rather more substantial objection relates specifically to reliance on tempo graphs: is it not dangerous to extrapolate from a single dimension of the musical performance to the whole? The answer is, of course, that it *is* dangerous, but then most attempts at explaining things involve taking risks. And here at least we have some support from Furtwängler, who attributed to tempo nuance the same kind of summarizing value that I previously discussed with reference to Brendel and Rink. (Indeed he went as far as to claim that "it is possible to tell from the treatment of the so-called *rubato*, as from a barometer reading, whether or not the impulses provoking it are in accordance with the real feeling of the passage or not, whether they are genuine or not.")[90] But in any case, just as we routinely analyze music on the basis of information that is less than perfectly reliable, so we routinely analyze it on the basis of highly incomplete representations: scores, for example.

In my view, however, there are some more serious objections to this kind of performance analysis, and in the remainder of this paper I shall state two of them. The first, which I can state but to which I do not have a reply, concerns the basic format of Figure 1. The vertical axis represents metronome values, but can one properly speak of a tempo when the values are constantly changing? Or to put the question the other way round, the shapes in the graph represent deviations from a notional steady tempo, but does the notional steady tempo have any phenomenological or psychological reality, and if not how can we justify speaking of deviations?[91] Should we maybe measure deviations not against a steady tempo in which the movement has probably never been performed, but against some grand average of the tempo profiles current at a particular time and place, insofar as they can be reconstructed from the recorded repertory? Or should we be understanding tempo profiles in a purely formal sense, without reference to any concept of deviation (and what exactly might that mean?). Since I do not know the answer to these questions, I shall pass on to the second objection, which will take longer to explain but to which I have a better idea of the answer.

---

90. Wilhelm Furtwängler (L. J. Lawrence, transl.), *Concerning Music*. Westport, Conn. 1977, p. 52.

This second objection involves a return to the opening concern of this paper, to words and music — or, in the terminology I used in the previous section, critical and performance interpretations. For if, as I have argued, it is misguided to look for an unproblematic translation of the one into the other, of analysis into performance, what kind of relationship *should* we expect to find between them? This question has been posed by the philosopher Jerrold Levinson,[92] according to whom it is a straightforward categorical error to think that a performance can ever embody a particular critical interpretation. Of course some performances are more compatible than others with a particular critical interpretation, he admits, but for any particular performance there could always be another compatible critical interpretation. For him, performances are always underdetermined with respect to critical interpretations, and so he concludes that "Even where a given PI might be said to correspond, in principle, to a particular theoretical understanding of a piece — and I think this is only rarely the case — it does not itself make that understanding available, nor is it good evidence of the possession of such an understanding on the part of the performer who offers it."[93] There seems, in short, to be a locked gate of difference between analysis and performance, although at the end of his article Levinson unbends as far as to concoct a reading of a movement from a Bach violin sonata that illustrates how critical analysis and performance might be connected with one another. But he immediately adds that "what I would emphasize (...) is just the contingency of most of these connections, and thus the implausibility of thinking that any sort of one-to-one correspondence can be demonstrated between given sets of performing choices and given critical conceptions in regard to a musical work."[94]

Levinson's demonstration is more satisfying logically than musicologically. One of the problems is that, in order to illustrate crit-

---

91. Eric Clarke begins to ask such questions in "Expression in Performance", pp. 23–24.
92. Jerrold Levinson, "Performative vs Critical Interpretation in Music", in: Krausz (ed.), *The Interpretation of Music*, pp. 33–60.
93. Ibidem, p. 41.
94. Ibidem, p. 59.

ical interpretations, he chooses non-technical appreciations of the old school (Philip Radcliffe, Antony Hopkins) in preference to the more analytically-informed and performance-oriented studies of, say, Joel Lester; in effect he ends up implying that what Lester does can't be done.[95] But then, if what I have said about translation (and what Levinson says about one-to-one correspondence) is correct, there is a sense in which what Lester does *can't* be done, or at least in which it involves a kind of systematic *mis*translation from one domain to the other. And yet it is by virtue of this kind of mistranslation that we can speak of performance at all. In this way, if there is indeed a locked gate of difference between words and music, it is evidently possible for meaning to squeeze between the bars. Or to put it more prosaically, it is not a question of analysis and performance converging to the point of identity, but of setting them off against one another, as Tim Howell implies when he speaks of encouraging performers "to play off intuitive responses against analytical perceptions in order to shape an interpretation".[96] But how far does my tandem analysis of Schenker and Furtwängler match up to this criterion? At the end of it I was careful to say that Furtwängler provided a 'correlate' of Schenker's spans, an 'equivalent' of his multi-level structures, and not a translation of them into performance, but is the difference in reality more than a play on words?

In essence I mapped Schenker's spans onto Furtwängler's tempo profiles. In other words, the analytical criterion was the fit or lack of fit between the two, although the process of mapping brought to light what might be termed a penumbra of difference between them. And if this enabled me to draw valid conclusions about the way in which Furtwängler created a distinctive bridge between analysis and performance, the viability of the project depended on a historically documented and quite exceptional bond between analyst and performer; of how many other top-ranking conductors

---

95. I have presented this argument at greater length in my review of Krausz's book (*Music and Letters* 77 (1996), pp. 103-109), where I suggest that if PIs are underdetermined with respect to CIs, then the reverse is also true.
96. Tim Howell, "Analysis and Performance: The Search for a Middelground", in: John Paynter *et al.*, *Companion to Contemporary Musical Thought*. London 1992, pp. 692-714, especially p. 698.

would a commentator be likely to comment that "his interpretation analyzed the structure"?[97] Moreover, my approach created a kind of complicity between subject and object, the most obvious symptom of which is the implicitly positive evaluation of Furtwängler and the way in which Mengelberg, as a less structurally-oriented interpreter, is set up as fall guy. (That in itself, of course, is reminiscent of Schenker's treatment of Leichtentritt.) In short, an analytical method which simply looks for fit or lack of fit between analysis and performance will necessarily fall short of the agenda which I outlined at the end of the previous section.

This situation is a not unfamiliar one in the analysis of performance, except that its results are sometimes less happy than in the alignment of Schenker and Furtwängler. An illuminating example (although one that must be reconstructed from the surviving documentation) is Webern's Piano Variations, of which Peter Stadlen gave the first performance under the composer's direction. Webern's directions were evidently comprehensive, as evidenced both by an article which Stadlen wrote twenty years later and by his performance score, heavily annotated in acccordance with Webern's instructions and subsequently published in transcription.[98] The motivation of Stadlen's article was polemical, but the annotated score supports his contention that Webern's performance directions were effectively unrelated to the music's serial organization. For instance, Webern asked Stadlen to bring out the notes at the top of the texture in the first movement, projecting them as a melody line. But the series is distributed homophonically, and therefore this melody line cuts right across it. Stadlen was not concerned to make sense of this (he was more interested in making nonsense of serialism), but a more recent commentator,

---

97. Peter Pirie, *Furtwängler and the Art of Conducting.* London 1980, p. 49. Not everybody agreed, of course; Paul Henry Lang wrote of "Furtwängler's inability to keep to a steady tempo", putting it down to "a certain lack of the sort of orchestral discipline we expect from our conductors" ("The Symphonies", in: *The Recordings of Beethoven as Viewed by the Critics from High Fidelity.* Westport, Conn. 1978, p. 22).
98. Peter Stadlen, "Serialism Reconsidered", in: *The Score* 22 (1958), pp. 12–27; Anton Webern, Piano Variations (Vienna 1979), Universal Edition 16845. I have discussed this example at greater length in "Analysing Performance, and Performing Analysis", pp. 249–250.

Robert Wason, is.[99] However Wason encounters a great deal of difficulty. After various abortive attempts to find some structure in the music that might justify such a performance interpretation, he suggests rather hopelessly that Webern's performance indications "point to structural features not immediately retraceable to the row [which] produce a tension against the structural segmentations, *while certainly assuming their existence*".[100]

Methodologically this conclusion is not a happy one. Either the performance interpretation is the same as the analysis (thereby confirming the analysis), or else it is different, in which case it confirms the analysis just by virtue of being different. If Webern's performance directions really did have nothing to do with the serial structure, there is no way you could discover it! For the theorist anxious at all costs to find *something*, this might be characterized as a win-win situation. But for the analysis of performance, it illustrates the poverty of a conceptual framework in which the only options are that p is the same as or similar to q on the one hand, and on the other that it isn't. Very much the same problems have long plagued the analysis of film music, for which traditional film theory had two categories: 'parallelism', meaning that music and film did the same, and 'counterpoint', meaning that they didn't. A further problem was that the film was assumed to be a semantically self-sufficient entity prior to the addition, normally at the last moment, of the music, giving rise to the paradoxical idea of inter-relating music and 'film' (paradoxical because the music is of course an element of the film). But such a conceptual framework is altogether inadequate for the rich variety of possible relationships between music, words, and pictures, or for the manner in which their mutual relationships contribute to the emergence of filmic meaning. More recent approaches[101] have not only significantly extended the analytical taxonomy of inter-media relationships, but also predicated an analytical process that models

---

99. Robert Wason, "Webern's *Variations for Piano*, Op. 27: Musical Structure and the Performance Score", in: *Integral* 1 (1987), pp. 57–103.
100. Ibidem, pp. 101–102 (emphasis mine).
101. See Nicholas Cook, *Analysing Musical Multimedia*. Oxford 1998, where further references may be found.

the way different media interact with one another in the construction of the overall experience. Instead of a prior meaning being mapped onto the music, the analysis effectively works from the bottom up.

I hope it is easy to see how readily all this maps onto the analysis of performance. As in the case of film, we have a dominant discourse (words and pictures, composed structure) which is mapped onto a marginalized one (film music, performance). In each case there is a one-way motion (film-to-music, analysis-to-performance), imposing a model according to which meaning is reproduced rather than emerging from the interaction, as I termed it in the previous section, of multiple agencies. Just as film theorists oppose 'film' and 'music', as if the latter were not already part of the former, so we talk about the relationship between 'music' and 'performance', as if music existed apart from performance. In each case, finally, we may recognize in the marginalized element a Derridean supplement, with all the deconstructive potential that that implies. Bringing performance into the mainstream of analysis, then, may involve some rethinking of established music-theoretical assumptions, but that is one of the reasons why it is worth doing. And the sooner we make a start on it the sooner the job will be done.

PERFORMANCE AND THE LISTENING EXPERIENCE: BACH'S "ERBARME DICH"

Peter Johnson

I. WORKS AND PERFORMANCES

THE WORK-CONCEPT

Perhaps the greatest impediment to the study of performance in Western art music is the assumption that the work actually or ideally predetermines the form of its performances. After all, if the correct or ideal performance could be read or imagined from the score, there would be little point in paying serious attention to individual performances, even if these were 'true' presentations of the composer's work. One can sympathise with the critic Ernest Newman who complained of having to leave his fireside to hear a second-rate performance when score-reading gave him "so much more pleasure".[1] It is through score-reading, Newman argues, that we know the work, yet "it reaches the plain man through the medium of a performer, and that medium may be a weak or even distorting one".[2] In *A Composer's World,* Hindemith pursues this theme to the logical conclusion that for music to depend upon a "performing mediator is an inherent weakness" of our art.[3] With the hindsight of contemporary hermeneutic and post-structuralist theory, it is elementary to track the fallacy of this argument to its initial premise, the *Werkkonzept*. The assumption that the work is fully predetermined and knowable from its score, its promotion as *opus perfectum ed integrum* such that any transformation is by definition a fall, is naïve in its idealism and pragmatically unworkable. The practice of composition and performance demonstrates

---

1. Felix Aprahamian, *More Essays from the World Music: Ernest Newman.* London 1958, p. 149.
2. Ibidem, p. 240.
3. Paul Hindemith, *A Composer's World.* Harvard 1951, p. 154. Hindemith's own international career as violist clearly counted for little once he had arrived at Yale.

beyond all doubt that compositions are made to be performed and that performance is an inherently interpretative art, from which it follows that performance as interpretation is an element *within* the intentionality of the work itself. To read a score as if it did not need performance, with all that the latter implies in terms of interpretation and recreation, is thus to deny one aspect of the work itself. Performance Studies allow the repositioning of work-orientated scholarship to include performance as a central factor in the ontology of the work. That this does not imply a weakening of the idea of the work, that it allows fresh and exciting reevaluations of the work as, for instance, an open text, is becoming increasingly apparent.

As Nicholas Cook has shown elsewhere in this volume, it has nonetheless been difficult for scholars nurtured in the traditional disciplines of historical musicology and analysis fully to escape the ideology of the work-concept. One critic to expose this problem was Joseph Kerman, who in the early 1980s earned considerable notoriety in the Anglo-American academic world by asking musicologists in general what they have offered "to the 'practical' world of music, the world of music performed, heard and recorded?"[4] Analysts are accused of 'myopia': their "dogged concentration on internal relationships within the single work of art is subversive as far as any reasonably complete view of music is concerned".[5] It is significant that Kerman's text has not been forgotten, and history may well condone the matter if not the manner of his critique.[6] It is not good enough for analysts to insist that their work informs performance if all that can be said is that the performer should articulate their particular readings: the point is ably demonstrated by Joel Lester, who shows that a Schenkerean analysis may, but need not, be articulated in performance. Why, Lester asks, should analysts not base their work on actual performances? "After all", he remarks, "most performers have in all likelihood devoted far more

---

4. Joseph Kerman, *Musicology*. London 1985, p. 185.
5. Ibidem, p. 73.
6. See for example the editors' preface in: Nicholas Cook and Mark Everist (eds.), *Rethinking Music*. Cambridge 1999, pp. v-xii.

time, care and training to realise music in sound than all but a few theorists."⁷ If the medium of analysis-through-performance is markedly different from that of the score-analyst, it is not necessarily less productive of insights into the work itself, as I hope to demonstrate in this chapter. And yet, for Lester, performance is still in certain respects a limitation, a foreclosing of the possibilities offered by the score, for while performances are 'richer' for adding "features never fully notated in any score", yet "each nuance limits the piece by excluding other options for that element. In this sense, a performance is necessarily only a single option for that piece, delineating some aspects while excluding others — just like a single analysis."⁸

A similar problem emerges in period instrument performance practice. Here the exchange between scholars and performers has been genuine and productive, yet this has arguably been bought at the cost of a false understanding of what performance can and should be. Peter Kivy has demonstrated that, in so far as there is but one correct performance under Authenticity, the latter is merely an extension of the *Werkkonzept* and therefore can allow no room for the performer's own voice.⁹ This does not challenge the artistic validity of the period instrument performance, but it does expose the fallacy of its claim to authenticity. Richard Taruskin has vigorously defended period instrument performance *against* the claims of authenticity by claiming that the real value of 'authentic' performances is that they are genuinely contemporary, they are *our* music. Period instrument musicians and singers interpret the ancient work "for their own time — that is for our time — the way all deathless texts must be reinterpreted if they are in fact to remain deathless and exempt from what familiarity breeds".¹⁰ In other words, it is the freshness of good period instrument performances, the way they cast familiar works in a new light or bring

---

7. Joel Lester, "Performance and Analysis: interaction and interpretation", in: John Rink (ed.), *The Practice of Performance*. Cambridge 1995, p. 198.
8. Ibidem, p. 199.
9. Peter Kivy, *Authenticities*. Cornell 1995.
10. Richard Taruskin, *Text and Act, Essays on Music and Performance*. Oxford 1995, p. 90.

to light the unfamiliar, that is so exciting, and it is the new materials and ways of reading the work that period instrument performance and its attendant musicology have made possible that empowers this avalanche of fresh insights. And yet, Taruskin's thesis applies equally to the imaginative mainstream performance, the value of which, arguably, rests in equal degree on its success in presenting the work in a fresh and vital interpretation. If Taruskin is right, the enduring musical work cannot be maintained as that which remains unchanged and unchanging. The picture emerges, rather, of the work as historically emergent, a function of its recent history of readings and performances.[11] The enduring work would then be the one that allows itself to be reinterpreted at different times and in different conditions, the one which diverse performers can find meaningful in their terms and which enables them to create that wonderful synthesis of structure and sonority, form and material we recognise as the outstanding performance *of* the fine musical work.[12]

It is one step from Taruskin's perceptive insight to Kivy's claim that the good performance should itself be valued as an art-work. Performance, Kivy declares, is like the art-work in being "the unique product of an individual, something with an individual style of its own, 'an original'".[13] He might have referred to Gadamer, who defined artistic work as "the creation of something exemplary which is not simply produced by following rules".[14] Kivy's intention is not to usurp the status of the notated musical work but to point to the necessary otherness of performance, the

---

11. José A. Bowen, "The History of Remembered Tradition: Tradition and its role in the relationship between musical works and their performances", in: *Journal of Musicology* 11 (1993), pp. 139–173. A parallel argument is developed by Hans Zender: "Interpretation — Schrift — Komposition", in: *Wir steigen niemals in denselben Fluss*. Freiburg 1996, pp. 59–82.
12. Adorno described Furtwängler's achievement as a conductor in terms of *Rettung*, meaning 'salvaging' or 'redemption': under his interpretative gaze, great works are regenerated. For discussion see Andrew Bowie, *From Romanticism to Critical Theory: The Philosophy of German Literary Theory*. London 1997, p. 189.
13. Kivy, *Authenticities*, p. 123.
14. Hans-George Gadamer, *The Relevance of the Beautiful and other essays* (Nicholas Walker, trans.). Cambridge 1986, p. 21.

fact that a performance must establish its own credentials as a meaningful and valued artistic act.[15] An entertaining, and perhaps tongue-in-cheek version of this thesis can be found in Proust. In *The Guermantes Way*, a performance by the idolized actress Berma is described in terms, not of authenticity to Racine, but of authenticity to the actress herself. Performance is "the momentary object, the mobile masterpiece which the art of the theatre intended". Berma's performance relates to *Phèdre* as a fine painting of a cathedral relates to the building — in both cases there is a pre-existent art-work which it falls to the practising artist to transcend through the creative act.[16] The musical performance, other than improvisation, is also figurative in this sense of investing a given object, the composer's work, in a particular material form, and, like the painting, this transformation can be routine or literal, or through technique, imagination, sensitivity and understanding can make its own claim to artistry. We shall see in Section 3 that Wagner makes a similar point: against the quotidian performance, the performance as art-work stands apart as an object to be valued and, thanks to recording, to be preserved. It is the special nature of the performance event, the 'extreme occasion' as Edward Said puts it, which ensures that, for the most part, performances are carefully prepared events, transcending their functionality in being fashioned as independent, responsible, artistic products that command attention *as* so-and-so's performance *of* the work and not simply the work in performance.[17]

---

15. For further discussion see Peter Johnson, "Musical Works, Musical Performances", in: *The Musical Times*, August 1997, p. 7.
16. Marcel Proust, *In Search of Lost Time, Part 3: The Guermantes Way* (C. K. Scott Moncrieff and Terence Kilmartin, trans., revised by D. J. Enright). London 1992, pp. 50–51. Proust's hero states the case for performance as art a good deal more strongly, for upon seeing Berma in an inferior play, he remarks: "I realized then that the work of the playwright was for the actress no more than the raw material, more or less irrelevant in itself, for the creation of her masterpiece of interpretation (...)", p. 50. This is of course to underplay the interrelationship between work and performance which is only fully satisfactory when both are of a high standard.
17. Edward Said, *Musical Elaborations*. New York 1991, Chapter 1. On the non-functionality of the art-work, see also Martin Heidegger, "The Origin of the Art-work", in: David Farrell Krell (ed.), *Basic Writings: Martin Heidegger*. London 1978, p. 171.

If the good performance transcends the work, we need to contemplate it in terms other than the ways in which it 'delineates some aspect' of the work. An immediate problem is to avoid the epistemological trap of reducing the performance to the concept, of denying what Adorno called its non-identity. How are we to value the individual performance *qua* art-work? William Rothstein offers intriguing possibilities in declaring performance to be 'a species of acting' and the performer's role 'to discover, or create, a musical narrative'. The key word here is 'create': performance becomes a matter not of explication but of the action of making. It follows, paradoxically, that the good performance *of* the work will assert its independence *from* the work in so far as the latter is predetermined: "a performance is not an *explication du texte*".[18] But, in that case, what is it? Rothstein speaks mysteriously of 'dramatic truth' and 'analytical truth', but what kind of discourse would allow access to the former without an unwarranted dependence upon the epistemological assumptions of the latter? What is urgently required is a strategy by which to engage with performance itself in terms that do not presuppose a given set of relationships to the score, without thereby losing sight of the obvious fact that the good performance is, always, a *bona fide* performance *of* the work. In proposing and illustrating such a strategy, I hope to show that the work does not thereby become redundant, but that the ways in which the good performance can be said to be 'of' the work are far removed from the traditional determinism of *Werktreue* and Authenticity.

METHODS (1)

The first task is to deconstruct the assumed epistemological dependence of the performance upon the work. The genitive relationship need not imply a strong determinism; indeed, if we were to set out to prove that performance must be fully predetermined by the work, we would need first to consider the two terms separately in order to demonstrate congruence. That this project has

---

18. William Rothstein, "Analysis and the Act of Performance", in: John Rink, *The Practice of Performance*, pp. 237-238.

not been attempted is indicative of the ideological grounding of determinism. Peter Kivy's notion of performance-as-art is promising if for no other reason than it breaks the umbilical cord subordinating performance to work without presupposing the real nature of the relationship. By regarding performances as "aesthetically important statements in themselves, not merely quotations of aesthetically important statements",[19] we are free to contemplate them as far as is possible in their own terms, just as every artwork demands to be contemplated in its own terms. This invites a method of approaching performance in which it is first 'read' as an independent 'aesthetic statement' and subsequently placed against other performances and readings of the work such that its individuality and its stylistic allegiances may emerge.

This method is not however unproblematic. It has been endemic in contemplating performance to invoke criteria which, as constituted, known facts, are strictly *a priori* to the performance itself. No wonder performance-criticism has tended to focus on the facile search for the (critic's) ideal performance, rather than a seeking of the informed evaluation of what a particular performance has to offer.[20] Jonathan Dunsby has even questioned whether we can know that the performances we have selected for study are in fact 'good' or worthy of critical attention.[21] Of course we cannot 'know' as a matter of proof, but the problem applies equally to the art-work itself: how do I know that Bach's aria "Erbarme dich" is itself worthy of study, or indeed, of repeated performances? Analysis will take us so far, but analysts rarely claim the authority to assert the value of the art-work. On the other hand, we know that the epistemological problems surrounding the question of value in art do not diminish our confidence in recognising the fine

---

19. Kivy, *Authenticities*, p. 118.
20. For a preliminary discussion of such concepts in the context of formal evaluation of performance see Peter Johnson, "Performance as Experience: the problem of assessment criteria", in: *British Journal of Music Education* 14/3 (1997), pp. 271–282.
21. Jonathan Dunsby, "Acts of Recall", in: *The Musical Times* (January 1997), p. 16. For a critical response see Peter Johnson, "Musical Works, Musical Performances", p. 7.

art-work; to this extent, art stands as a permanent reminder of the limitations of epistemology itself.[22]

The finest performances also resemble the art-work in transcending their use-value. In so far as one function of performance is to sound out the composer's score, the artistic performance transcends this functionality, just as Proust's painting of a cathedral is both representational and also assertive of its own artistic value. Far from being the one that most faithfully 'presents' the work according to preconceived notions of how that should be done, the finest performance or painting may be the one that transcends the original without seeming to transgress whatever inherent properties we read in it.[23] In other words, to acknowledge the artistry in performance demands the reversal of our conventional theorising of the work/performance relationship: we should ask of the finest performances how they *exceed* the work, or, perhaps, how they deconstruct it.

A more pressing problem is the impossibility of the strictly neutral position. Nattiez's 'neutral level' of score-analysis is problematic for this reason.[24] In the case of a performance of a familiar work, the critic can hardly ignore other performances which may have seemed exemplary or that ideal reading which every competent score-reader seems able to imagine. We are, as Heidegger claimed, already engaged, already within the hermeneutic circle. Joseph Kerman is one of the very few musicologists to acknowledge such influence. He closes his discussion of the slow movement of

---

22. For a comprehensive analysis see Theodor Adorno, *Negative Dialectics* (E.B. Ashton (trans.), *Negative Dialektik*). London 1973, especially Part 2: "Concept and Categories": "Nothing in the world is composed — added up, so to speak — of factuality and concept", p. 188.
23. José A. Bowen argues that the validity of a performance as a *bona fide* presentation of the work is culturally contingent to the extent of being legitimated by no-one but the current audience: "Tempo, Duration and Flexibility", p. 128.
24. Jean-Jacques Nattiez, *Music and Discourse: Towards a Semiology of Music* (Carolyn Abbate, trans.). Princeton 1990, p. 11. Nattiez's recognition that performance itself constitutes a 'text', supported by its own poiesis, including the work as source, and its esthesis provides a useful theoretical framework for performance study.

Beethoven's Op. 135 with a reference to Toscanini's famous arrangement for the strings of the NBC orchestra. To the purist, Kerman remarks, Toscanini's performances were "sufficiently horrifying", and yet "the impression is unforgettable, and while such memories remain, one can never be sure about the freshness of one's critical response".[25] There is a prescience of postmodernism in Kerman's remark, an honest recognition that a neutral score-reading or analysis may be as idealistic as the ideal performance and that, as interpretative acts, both are marked by the cultural contextualisation of their *poiesis*.

MUSIC AS SOUND

A degree of neutrality in our 'readings' of performance might be better assured if we understood the nature of the performer's unique contribution to the performed art-work. What is it, specifically, that the performer achieves as distinct from the composer? A familiar thesis is that the performer converts the spatial or relational score-elements into real time, and in so doing introduces subtle inflexions. These indeed have been exposed by, among others, David Epstein, Bruno Repp and José Bowen.[26] I shall return to the question of tempo and timing in Section 3, but a more pressing problem concerns the physical properties of musical sound itself, the secrets of which performance study has barely begun to penetrate.

It is this rich and complex world of physical sound that is absolutely closed to score-reading, for the very simple fact is that it does not exist until the performer touches string with bow, or reed with lips, or activates the vocal chords from within his or her body to generate sounding music. This sound differs from the imagined, virtual sound of a score-reading in being proper to the performer. However vivid and realistic imagined music may be, it

---

25. Joseph Kerman, *The Beethoven Quartets*. Oxford 1967, p. 223.
26. David Epstein, *Shaping Time: Music, the Brain, and Performance*. Schirmer 1995; Patrick Shove and Bruno Repp, "Musical Motion and Performance: theoretical and empirical perspectives", in: Rink, *The Practice of Performance*, p. 55; Bowen, "Tempo, Duration and Flexibility". See also Nicholas Cook's discussion in this volume.

exists outside the physical domain of experienced sound; it is constituted not as transcendence of sound but in the absence of sound. Neither is the score-reader publically accountable for virtual sounds: virtual sounds are already the signifieds of the score-signs, already deeply embedded in the intentionality of reader-interpretation. The real sounds of performed music, on the other hand, impinge upon the ear and mind of the listener as strictly *other*, strictly objective. It is because they are external that they themselves demand interpretation. In other words, whereas the score as text is interpreted by the score-reader as an ideal music constituted of virtual sound as the signifieds of the score-signs, performance is constituted by the listener from physical sound as signifier, constituting the fabric of the music. To conflate the two, to assume that score-reading is a kind of performance, is to deny the power of sound itself as creatively managed in performance.[27] The performer's task, therefore, is to generate sound according to, yet always transcending, the score-signs.[28] This is not to underestimate the importance of the composer, but merely to value the performer's complementary art in attending to aspects of that music which are quite beyond the composer's control. Performance is a function of the performer's unique individuality as a practising musician engaged in reading and interpreting the composer's work as he or she feels to be right for the particular circumstances of the present moment.

An immediate consequence of the presentness of performance is the extent to which prepared interpretations or score-readings may need to be adjusted to suit present contingencies. There is nothing unartistic about this; indeed, Richard Wollheim argues that

---

27. Suzanne Langer argued on these grounds that performance is the 'natural completion' of the art-work, which of course presupposes the work to be fully constituted, a given: Suzanne Langer, *Feeling and Form*. London 1953, p. 146. I do not suggest that there is no boundary between work and performance, merely that its drawing is itself an interpretative act. See Bowen, "Tempo, Duration and Flexibility" for further discussion.

28. Boulez writes that "scores are diagrams it is imperative to 'realize' — to bring into concrete existence (...)", in: P. Boulez, *Orientations: Collected writings* (J.-J. Nattiez, ed., Martin Cooper, trans.). Faber & Faber 1986, p. 33. See also Nicholas Cook in this volume.

every artistic production involves the subordination of intention to the pragmatics of realisation. He thus reads every art-work in terms of a mediation or 'testing' between intention and the resistance of the materials themselves. "In the case of art, this testing occurs twice over: first, in the confrontation of the artist and his medium, and then again in the confrontation of the artist and his society. On both occasions it is characteristic that the artist surrenders something that he cherishes in response to the stringencies of something that he recognizes as external to, and hence independent of, himself."[29]

Such a process of testing can explicitly be traced in the compositional methods of a Beethoven or a Birtwistle, but it is evident too in the daily practice routines of the performer. Karajan stated that, however carefully the conductor mentally prepares the score, it is only when the conductor hears the sounds of the orchestra that interpretation begins in earnest. For the pianist, too, "the moment you come to play, the moment when you feel the pressure of the whole body on the keys, that is when the real process of interpretation really begins".[30] To this extent, the good performer must respond flexibly and creatively at the moment of performance, and it is in this way that the good performance transcends the merely routine presentation. To this extent each performance is a unique event, which does not mean that performances, as types, are not repeatable. It is because Authenticity denies this present negotiation between intention and actual physical sound that Peter Kivy can complain that, whereas we used to have as many *Goldberg Variations* as there were performances of the work, under Authenticity there was but one *Goldberg Variations*, namely the ideal performance, ideal since to be 'correct' it could not have been subject to this process of 'testing' as a 'confrontation' of artist and the physical and social worlds of the emergent performance.[31]

---

29. Richard Wollheim, *Art and its Objects*. London 1968, p. 133.
30. Richard Osborne, *Conversations with Karajan*. Oxford 1989, p. 94.
31. Kivy, *Authenticities*, p. 278.

METHOD (2)

One starting point for performance study is consequently the sounds as generated in actual performance, just as the use of paint and brush-stroke offers one important route towards an understanding of a painting. Yet what is musical sound? In so far as sound has material and measurable properties, it lends itself to acoustic analysis which, as we shall see, can bring to light certain properties of the music we hear. Nonetheless, if music transcends its sounds, it does so in the mind of the listener.[32] The results of acoustic analysis need careful handling, both because the inner ear processes sound somewhat differently from our scientific instruments, and because, beyond the listening lies the constituted musical experience itself, the point at which musical sound becomes music. The listener, and the subjectivity of listening, are therefore critical factors in any study of performance, for it is through the act of listening that living music is constituted from physical sound. The complexity of this process is evident: if the listener has studied the score or heard the work in other performances, the perceived sounds will be constituted against a set of assumptions about how the work or the performance 'is' or should be. It falls to the performer to persuade the listener that the present performance is worthy of the time and effort of attention, or that, for the moment, the present performance can ideally be *taken as* definitive. Edward Said elegantly captures this perceptual property of the good performance: "What interests me is the way the best interpreters of poetry and music allow both their audience and themselves (self conviction not being the least of an interpreter's virtues) the proposition that the work being presented is *as if* created by the performer. Somehow the work appears to gain its justification, its rightness, its *thereness* in the words of Sergiu Celibidache, by that interpretation (...). This is of course an illusion."[33]

---

32. On the limitations of acoustic analysis in capturing the listening experience, see Hans Zender, "Über das Hören", in: *Happy New Ears*. Freiburg 1997(1991), p. 18.
33. Said, *Elaborations*, p. 89.

Neither should we hasten to accuse performance of perpetrating the mere illusion, for, as we shall see in Section 3, every art-work is in important respects illusory.

Since performance specifically relies upon the subjective act of listening, the problem of subjectivity itself cannot be evaded. However, the listening response itself is not, or need not be, purely solipsistic, as is evident from the experience of performance itself. If performers from different continents can meet for rehearsal in the morning, and the same evening broadcast a performance round the world that is meaningful to an international audience, the empirical case for a high level of intersubjective accord in our music-making and listening is very strong. This of course depends both upon the public validity of the individual listening experience and upon the reproducibility of the fine adjustments to nuance that are worked out in rehearsal, and upon which the artistry of the performance depends in large measure. Audiences and critics, likewise, engage in intersubjective exchanges at various levels from the purely somatic to the critically discursive. In fact, performance study will expose the fallacy of the subject/object dichotomy itself, not by denying the objectivity or otherness of music-in-sound (that which can be recorded) nor the subjectivity of the listener's experience of the music, but by accommodating the dialectical interdependence of each upon the other. "Subjective and objective aesthetics are equally exposed to the critique of a dialectical aesthetics: the former because it is either abstractly transcendental or arbitrary in its dependence on individual taste; the latter because it overlooks the objective mediatedness of the art by the subject."[34]

Adorno thus argues that the art-work should be contemplated neither in exclusively objective terms, valuable as these may be, nor in exclusively subjective terms: a Third Way is clearly required. I propose that this can be found through a dialectic of objective and subjective approaches, each informing the other in what will

---

34. Theodor Adorno, *Aesthetic Theory* (Robert Hullot-Kentor, trans.). The Athlone Press 1997, p. 166. (Gretel Adorno and Rolf Tiedemann (eds.), *Ästhetische Theorie*. 1970).

emerge as a hermeneutical discourse firmly grounded upon what is actually discernible in the performance as text. Accordingly, I illustrate, in Section 2, certain techniques of acoustic analysis, pointing out that no set of data can be regarded as musically meaningful until it has been interpreted or correlated with anterior musical experience; in Section 3, I consider the problem of experience and subjectivity, and will conclude that analysis offers a valuable method of understanding that which we have already experienced, and of sharpening that experience. My thesis is that we should celebrate performance for the experience it offers *through* the medium of the work, rather than cling to the false image of the idealised work, transparently manifest through the medium of performance. Performance analysis thus exposes the work in a new and fascinating light, as a text allowing rich and varied opportunities for the imaginative performer.

II. THE ANALYSIS OF PERFORMANCE: "ERBARME DICH".

FREQUENCY SPECTRA AND TUNING

We must expect, therefore, for the physical properties of the imaginative performance, which are the properties of its sounds as interpreted by the sensitive listener, to deconstruct the way the work has previously been heard and understood. The history of the reception of period instrument performances provides a test-case for this process, and I have accordingly selected two recordings of the aria "Erbarme dich" from the *Matthäus-Passion* (No.39), one from the recent mainstream tradition and one period instrument performance. This aria has been selected on account of Naomi Cumming's splendid score-analytical account, to which I refer in some detail in Section 3. My selected performances are from Karl Richter's 1980 LP record with the Munich Bach Choir and Orchestra, and John Eliot Gardiner's 1987 CD with the Monteverdi Choir and English Baroque Soloists.[35] I refer to the recordings as 'KR' and 'JEG' respectively. I shall concentrate on the first eight bars.

---

35. The Richter LP is on DGG 413 939-1, the Eliot Gardiner CD is on Archiv 427648-1/2/4.

Spectral and spectrographic analysis have long been meat and drink for researchers in music technology and sound synthesis, but musicologists have been reluctant to draw on the considerable analytical resources available. The mathematical theory is undoubtedly daunting, but the plots and graphs are not difficult to read and interpret, and I shall introduce them in non-technical terms.[36] It is important to note that charts and graphs represent a transposition from the domain of digitised sound to the visual. The reader needs to make a second transposition from the visual to the musical, for graphs such as these have no musical meaning until interpreted.[37] The claim to objectivity of any such method is therefore compromised. Indeed, what is shown is subject to the limitations generic to the system — this is the standard caveat of any scientific test. Like a musical score, our charts and graphs suggest types of musical sound, but only to the experienced reader. The reader is therefore urged to compare these visual images with the recorded performances they represent.

Figure 1 represents the accumulated energy over approximately the first six beats in each recording, frequency being plotted along the x- or horizontal axis.[38] Pitch-names and exact frequency are shown against the more significant peaks, these being automatically generated by the software to show the exact frequency of the peak and display it together with its pitch-name. In JEG, pitch-names are

Example 1: Bach, "Erbarme dich" (Matthäus-Passion) BWV 244, No.39), bars 1-2; reduction from Bärenreiter miniature score, TP196 (n.d.)

---

36. All the plots shown in this paper use customized forms of the Signal Processing and plotting software in Matlab.
37. Bowen, "Tempo, Duration and Flexibility", p. 113.
38. Technically, this is a plot of 'power spectrum density', showing the accumulated power across the frequency spectrum. Logarithmic conversion converts power to amplitude, shown in decibels.

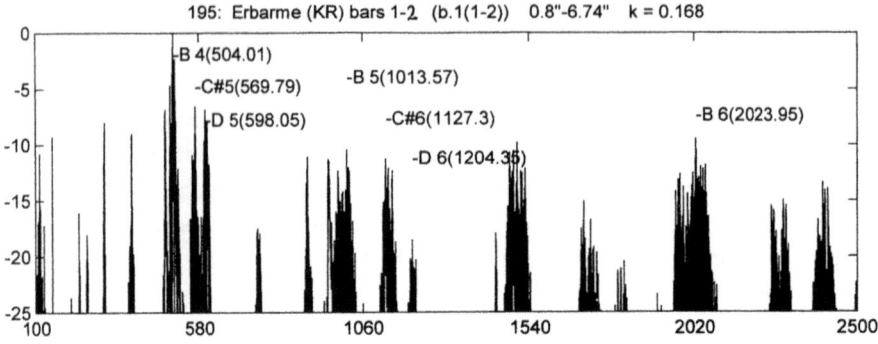

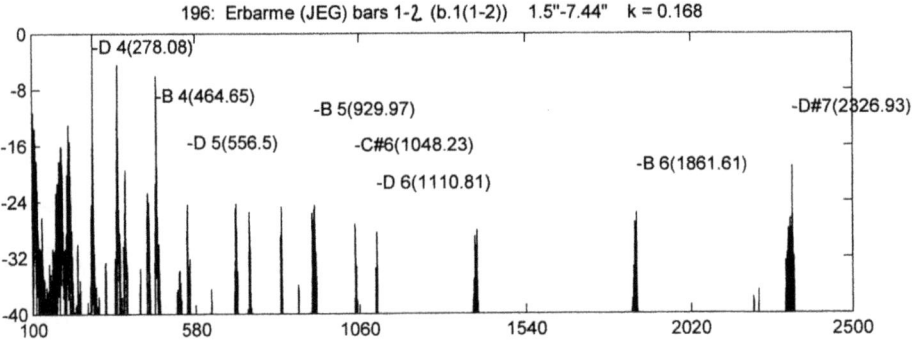

Figure 1:
Bach, "Erbarme dich",
(Matthäus-Passion
No.39), bars 1–2:
Frequency analysis.
Frequency (Hertz) v.
Decibels from the peak
reading.

adjusted to allow for A = 415 tuning. Frequency is given to two decimal places, although the maximum error is <0.168Hz. The question of precision is very important, although rarely discussed in the musical literature on spectral analysis. 0.168 is the value of a constant I designate as k, shown to the right of the title on each plot. I shall shortly explain the derivation of this constant, but for the moment it is sufficient to grasp that frequency in these analyses is plotted in increments of k. In other words, the graph should be plotted as a bar-chart where the width of each bar is kHz. We shall see that k, and hence the precision of the readings, needs to be adjusted according to the specific purpose of the analysis.

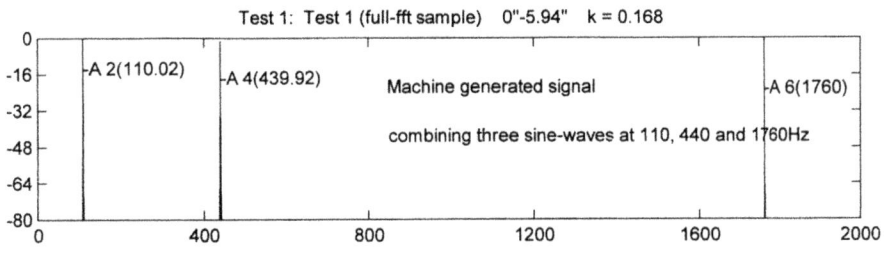
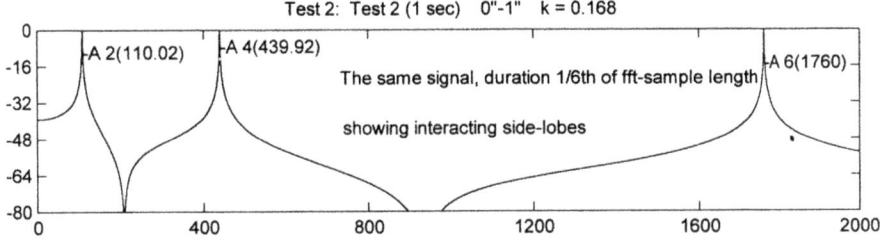
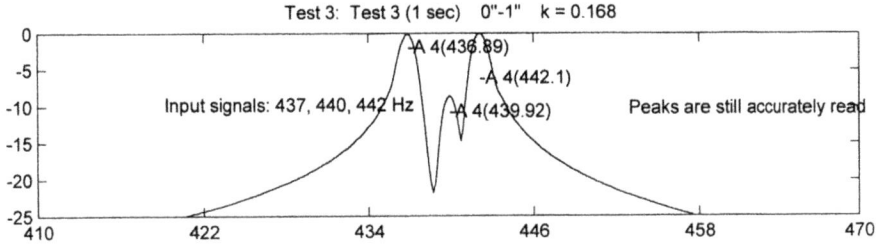

To illustrate the level of precision in my methods, Figure 2 shows three test plots. The two upper plots analyse the frequency-content of an identical computer-generated signal comprising three sine-waves of 110, 440 and 1760Hz, i.e. a rather 'flutey' $a2$.[39] Frequency readings are shown for each peak and emerge as identical in the two plots. They deviate slightly, however, from the known frequencies in the signal because they show the integer

Figure 2: Tests: Frequency analyses of machine-generated signals showing side-lobes. Frequency (Hertz) v. Decibels from the peak reading.

---

39. I adopt the American standard for the description of pitch-names: c2 is the cello c-string, b1 the note below; c4 is thus 'middle C', a4 corresponds to A=440; soprano C is c6.

multiples of k nearest to the real frequency. Thus, the peak at 440Hz falls within the band starting at 439.92 (k x 2615), and no more accurate reading is available with this setting of k.[40]

The value of k is of considerable importance. It is determined by the simple proportion between *sample-rate*, which in all my data-samples is set at 22.05kHz (one half the standard CD rate), and the *sample-size*, the number of samples used for the analysis. In Figures 1 and 2, the sample-size was set to 2^{17} or 131072. Thus:

$$k = \text{sample-rate}/\text{sample-size} = 22050/131072 = 0.1682.$$

In Figure 3, however, *sample-size* will be set at 2^9 or 512, giving a value of k of 22050/512 = 43.07. Had we used that value for the analysis plotted in Figure 1, frequency would have been plotted in steps of c. 43Hz, giving intolerably low precision, at least for the lower frequency-range. We shall learn shortly why the higher setting of k is sometimes necessary.

The lower two plots in Figure 2 expose a different problem. While the upper plot used a length of signal commensurate with the size of the analysed sample (5.94s is $1/k$), in the lower two plots, the system assumed the long *sample-size* of 2^{17} samples, while being supplied with only one second's worth, i.e. 22050 samples. The program responds by *zero padding* the file to the required *sample-size*, thus generating a file the size of *sample-size*, which is then analysed. The reason for this artifice is to preserve the accuracy of frequency reading by keeping k very low, and hence *sample-size* as high as possible. The middle plot in Figure 2 shows the consequences: using the same test signal as in the upper plot, each of the peaks is represented to the correct degree of precision, but broad curving lines extend from the lower levels of the peak signals and interact (as sums) to form an apparent carpet of background noise which we know from the upper plot is not in the original signal. These curves are known as 'side-lobes' and are mathematically predictable.[41] They do not affect the peak-readings, and become troublesome only at relatively low amplitude

---

40. Small apparent discrepancies in such calculations are caused by rounding.
41. A very slight broadening of the signal towards the base can also be detected in the upper plot, and side-lobes cannot wholly be eradicated. A filter or 'window' is conventionally used to minimize the effect. All my plots use the Hanning Window.

levels: the y-scaling in the middle plot extends to absurdly low levels. The bottom plot shows what happens when peaks are very close together: the peaks are never absorbed into side-lobes, but a false impression is given of sound-bands connecting the peaks at lower decibel levels.

The lower plot also tests the analysis of differential amplitude-levels, for in the test signal the middle frequency was set at 1/3rd of the intensity of the two outer ones. The result is about a 10 decibel drop, corresponding to the ear's logarithmic analysis of amplitude difference.

Returning to Figure 1, the upper plot (KR) shows considerable width of frequency, especially in the region of the higher harmonics such as *b6*. This is clearly not caused by side-lobes since the full *sample-size* of 5.94s is used; discrete peaks rather than curving lines are visible, too, even at the edges of the band. I shall shortly demonstrate that this effect is indicative of the frequency spread of vibrato. Another contributory factor to these wide bands is undoubtedly the combining of harmonics from solo violin with various notes and harmonics of the accompanying strings and organ, although, as the lower plot (JEG) shows, remarkable consistency of intonation is possible even over a six-second extract. The open, clean appearance of JEG, even with the y-axis extended to -40dB, contrasts sharply with the upper plot.

Figure 1 also illustrates how intonation may be measured. Let us take JEG first and compare the *d5* (556.50Hz) with the *b4* (464.65Hz). A pure minor third would be an exact ratio of 6:5 between the upper and lower frequencies. The calculation, from the *b4* peak, is:

Pure *d5* from *b4* (JEG): 464.65 x 6/5 = 557.58Hz

This is about 0.2% deviation from the actual *d5* peak at 556.50, with a margin of error of k x 6/5 = 0.20Hz. Converting the difference logarithmically to cents (where 100 cents = one equal-tempered semitone) gives a deviation of 3.36 cents flatter than pure, with a margin of error <0.06 cents.[42] For comparison, the equal-

---

42. It is necessary to work in cents to equalise intervallic relationships at any frequency level. The difference between frequencies f1 and f2 is 1200 x log2 (f2/f1) cents.

tempered minor third is about 15.7 cents flat. This compares interestingly with KR. The equivalent calculations in the latter are:

Pure *d5* from *b4* (KR): 504.01 x 6/5 = 604.81Hz

a difference of 6.76Hz from KR's tuning at 598.05Hz, or 19.5 cents flat. Listening confirms that the main energy of the *d5* comes from the solo violin, and we can thus confirm that the soloist is tuning this note 1/5th of a semitone flatter than pure, and significantly flatter even than equal temperament. I would hasten to point out that these results should not be used for evaluative purposes; KR's 19.5 cents flat tuning of *d5* does not *sound* out of tune, and these results suggest that expressive tuning is being used. Expressive tuning is occasionally mentioned in the performance literature, for example by Casals, and there is some psycho-acoustic research into this phenomenon.[43] I do not pursue this question here, but these and other results suggest that a thorough investigation into string intonation could be undertaken by this method.

SPECTROGRAMS

The frequency plots in Figures 1 and 2 condense data gathered across the given time-span into single readings for each frequency-band, so that frequency-variation within the time-span is not analysed, and is suggested only by the width of the signals. To plot variation of frequency over time we need a more complex procedure, one that is, however, not entirely unproblematic. Figure 3 shows spectrograms for the first two bars in each of KR's and JEG's recordings. Here, frequency is plotted on the y-axis, so that horizontal strips represent sustained frequencies. Time is plotted

---

43. Casals is clear that what he terms 'expressive tuning' is in fact a performative response to syntax, as for example by sharpening the rising leading-note: David Blum, *Casals and the Art of Interpretation*. California 1977, pp. 102–109. My studies (unpublished) are generating mounting evidence that string players frequently reverse this tendency (i.e. flatten the rising leading-note below a 'pure' or just tuning), suggesting a more explicitly 'expressive' as distinct from 'syntactical' approach to intonation than Casals (or Blum) allowed. For a psychological paper on the perception of tuning and its association with affective response see Scott Makeig, "Affective versus analytical perception of musical intervals", in: Manfred Clynes (ed.), *Music, Mind, and Brain: the Neuropsychology of Music*. New York & London 1982, p. 227.

on the x-axis, and amplitude represented by the intensity of colour at each point in the graph. A spectrogram is in fact a series of vertical strips, each representing a frequency plot comparable to Figure 1, rotated through ninety degrees. Instead of peaks and troughs, the plot shows amplitude variation by different colours.[44] The width of each vertical strip is once again set by k. In fact, this plot is a representation of a matrix of discrete readings of size k x k, except that only half of the frequency-readings are usable so that the frequency is plotted from 0Hz to a maximum of *sample-rate*/2, which, here, is about 11kHz. Higher frequencies can be accessed only by resampling the original sound-file at a higher rate.[45]

What immediately emerges is the timbral shaping in the lower plot, where JEG's violinist (probably Elizabeth Willcock) allows the very high harmonics to emerge only at the centre of the tones. This is the characteristic *messa di voce* of Baroque string playing, and an effect particularly prominent in the second bar (*g5, a5*). Note here that the prominent harmonics are evenly spaced and therefore pertain to the same fundamental frequency which will be the perceptually dominant pitch. Since higher fundamentals will produce more widely spaced harmonics than lower fundamentals, it is possible to track the shape of the melody by the widening or narrowing bands (from the 9 sec. point, for instance, the prominent harmonics are those of *g5, a5* and *f#5* respectively). Little further information can be gleaned directly from these plots, but a wealth of detail can be exposed by rescaling or by calling up the digital data in different forms. Figures 4 and 5 illustrate some of the possibilities.

Figure 4 shows a close-up of Figure 3 in which two distinct frequency bands are shown over a reduced time-span. These bands represent two harmonics of the sustained *b5* in the second half of

---

44. The same data can be represented by a contour plot, where isometric amplitude levels are plotted as contour lines, as is altitude on a map, and 3-D plots are also available. Such plots are more appealing visually but rarely reveal explicit analytical data.
45. The primary reason for this limitation is that full-length Fourier Transforms are symmetrical on the frequency axis. The maximum available frequency is the 'Nyquist' frequency, given by (sample-rate/2) - 1.

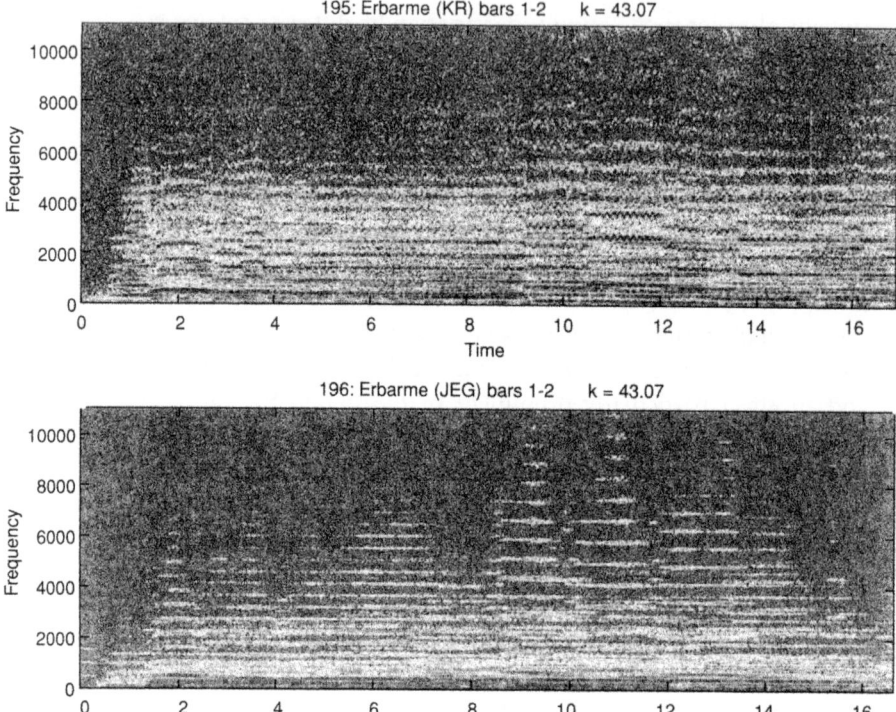

Figure 3:
"Erbarme dich",
bars 1–2: Spectrograms.
Time in seconds,
frequency in Hertz.

performance and the listening experience

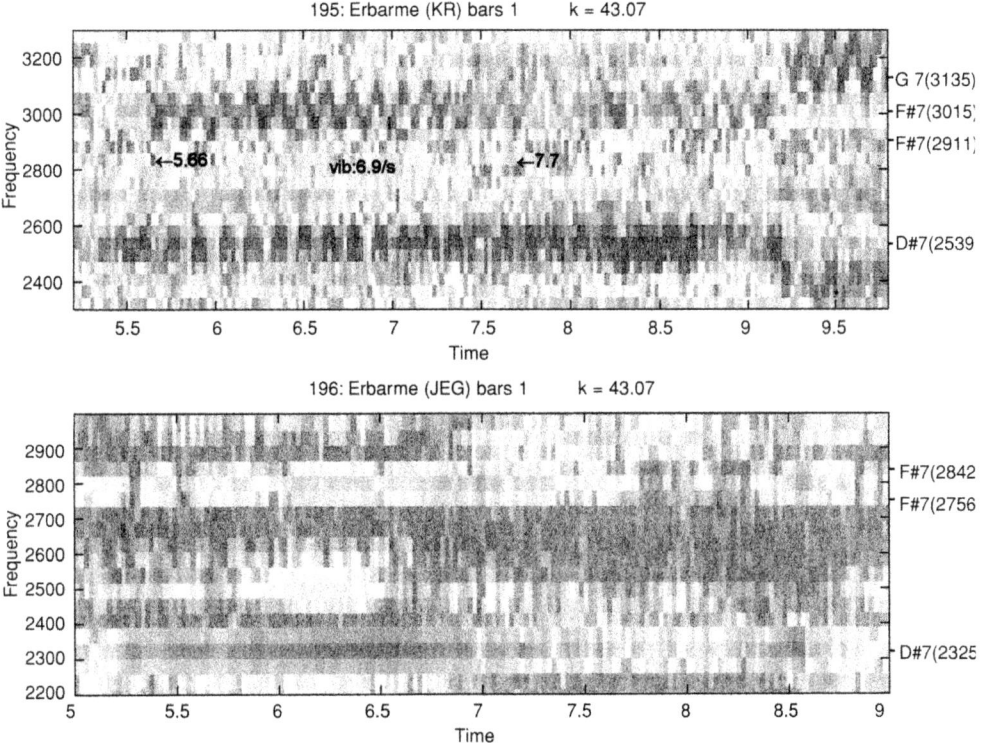

Figure 4:
"Erbarme dich",
bars 1-2: Close-up of
Figure 3.

bar 1, the fifth at *d#7* and the sixth, *f#7*. The shift of harmony in the last beat of bar 1 is clearly visible at about 7.5s in the upper plot and at about 7s in the lower, JEG adopting a noticeably faster tempo than KR. The final 0.5s or so in Figure 4 represent the start of the next bar, fresh harmonics arising from the solo violin's rise to *g5* and the change of harmony. The differences in texture and playing style are clearly illustrated here. KR's violinist sustains the tone with an intensification towards the end of the bar at approximately 9.2s. JEG's violinist allows a crescendo on the fifth harmonic *d#5* but there is an equally marked falling away over a period of some 1.3s just where KR's violinist increases amplitude. As in our discussion of intonation, this data strongly invites interpretation.

In Figures 3 and 4, the sample-size was set at 2^9 so that

$$k = 22050/512 = 43.0664$$

Why the change from Figure 1, and why in particular the loss of accuracy in the frequency domain such that each frequency-step is now a full 43Hz? The problem is that while frequency $f \sim k$, time $t \sim 1/k$, so that in order to represent the time-domain to a level of precision commensurate with the ear's ability to discriminate rapid changes, we need a high value of k. This 'difference limen', dL, is generally taken as c. 20–30ms (0.02-0.03 seconds) for the average competent listener, though it may be less for the experienced performer.[46] Thus, for a string of notes played at MM. 200, where each note lasts about 0.3s, psycho-acoustical research suggests that the ear could in theory detect ten events within each note. It is of course not quite that simple, for Gestalt processes tend to smooth small irregularities; however, the perception of fine nuances of timing can be cultivated by ear-training such as is demanded of high-level performance on non-keyboard instruments. With k set at 43.07, the margin of error in the time-domain is $<1/k = 0.023$, giving sufficient precision for most purposes. This explains why a single comprehensive print-out, corresponding in

---

46. For a full account and experimental data on how this affects perception of asynchrony, see Albert S. Bregman, *Auditory Scene Analysis: the Perceptual Organization of Sound.* MIT 1994. See also Epstein, *Shaping Time*, p. 143.

performance and the listening experience

both the frequency and time-domains to the acuity of the human ear, is not available: two plots are necessary as illustrated in Figures 1 and 2 and Figures 3 and 4 respectively.

Figure 4 shows some striking differences between the visual images in KR and JEG which obviously correspond to the acoustic phenomena. The upper plot shows vibrato as a regular oscillation about a mean frequency, whereas the lower plot shows some width in the signal, but no apparent oscillation of frequency. In KR, vibrato is particularly marked between the 5.6s and 7.7s markers,[47] and from this plot, vibrato rates can be measured directly.[48] Thus, the frequency-spread for this harmonic appears, at most, to be between 2911 and 3135Hz, namely approx. 128 cents, a spread of one-and-a-quarter semitones. However, given the 43Hz margin of error in frequency-readings here, and the possible effect of side-lobes which may appear on the spectrogram as faint images shadowing the peak signals, we cannot be sure how perceptually prominent the outer edges of the zig-zag line are for the listener. More accurate readings of vibrato-spread can be taken by examining very high harmonics (in order to off-set the 43Hz margin of error) in combination with frequency plots such as Figure 1, which gives very accurate analysis of frequency. Examination of *f#7* in a frequency plot (not shown) suggests that a frequency spread of 120 cents is an overestimation, and that frequency variation is of the order of 100 cents. By these methods, frequency spread at this harmonic can be shown to be not less than 100 cents or one semitone. This is in fact a modest vibrato-spread, mainstream singers characteristically covering at last 2 semitones or 200 cents in a standard vibrato-cycle, and occasionally as much as a perfect fourth (500 cents!).

---

47. In the figures, time-points are read on the vertical axis indicated by the tip of the left-hand arrow. These are read automatically by the soft-ware from the cursor positon on the monitor and are therefore subject to scaling in the monitor image.

48. I use 'vibrato' to refer to periodic changes in both frequency and amplitude. Instrumentalists and vocalists in fact tend to invert the use of 'vibrato' and 'tremolo', and it is rare to find an occurrence of 'f-vibrato' without 'a-vibrato' (flautists tend to use the latter exclusively, singers the former). There is also spectral vibrato, the periodic presence and absence of certain harmonics, a standard feature of the vibrato on the oboe.

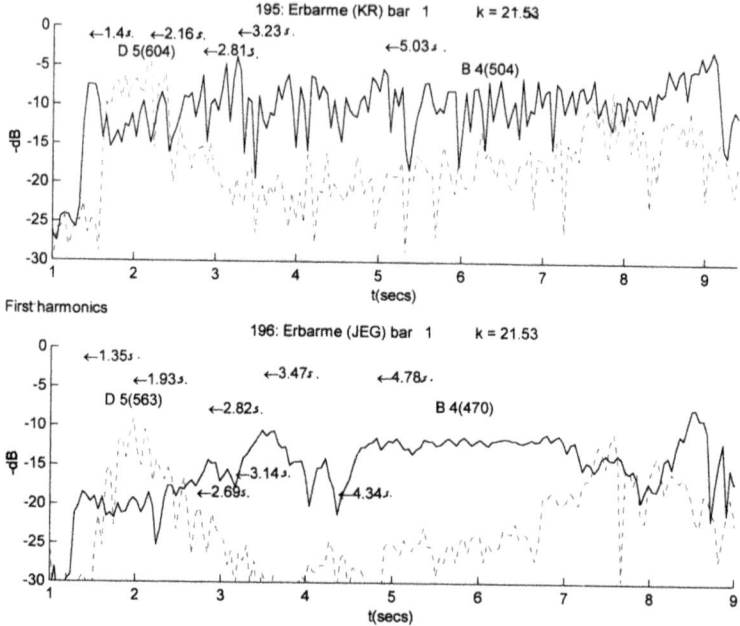

Figure 5: *"Erbarme dich", bars 1-2: Single fundamental frequency bands (from Fig. 3). Amplitude variation against time.*

Vibrato-rate, the number of cycles per second (cps), can also be measured from Figure 4 by counting the number of cycles over a given time. By this method, readings vary between 6.8 and 6.9cps, giving a safe average of 6.85 cps. This is considerably faster than the singers' characteristic vibrato-rate, which rarely exceeds 5.5cps and is often much less.[49] The lower plot, however, suggests that there is no measurable vibrato in JEG. This can be checked by examining the data in even more detail.

In Figures 5 and 6, single horizontal strips have been extracted from Figure 4 and plotted in two dimensions to show the variation of amplitude over time for each chosen frequency-band. We remember that each band represents a discrete frequency-range of width *k*Hz. In the upper plot of Figure 5, we see the content of two rows from the data-file from which Figures 3 and 4 are constructed. They are in fact the 23rd and the 28th rows, which, scaled

---

49. This discussion draws on unpublished research data.

performance and the listening experience

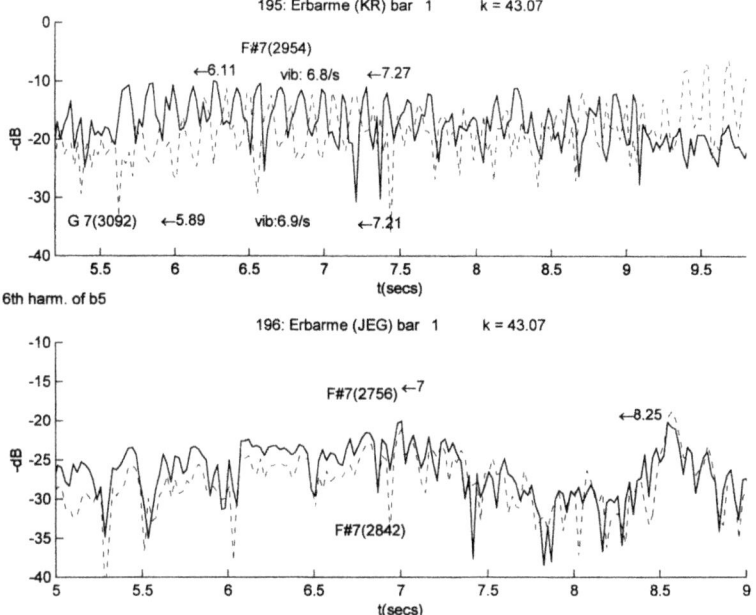

Figure 6:
"Erbarme dich", bars 1-2
Frequency bands over the
sixth harmonic of b5
(cf. Figures 5 and 3).

by *k*, give frequencies corresponding to *b4* and *d5* respectively (note the new value of *k*, adjusted to improve definition in the frequency domain, but with corresponding reduction of accuracy in the time-domain to c. 46ms). The differences between the two plots in Figure 4 are immediately apparent. The falling away of tone in the lower plot towards the bar line at c. 8s confirms our observation from Figure 3, and the articulation of the respective *b4*s in the first three beats of bar 1 is clearly visible. These are indicated by time-points to be read from the tip of the left-pointing arrows. Thus, the peaks at *b4* are at 1.35s, 2.82s, a large peak at 3.47s and a sustained high amplitude level starting at 4.78 and ending at about 7s. The first of these is markedly weaker than that of the initial *d5*, plotted as a dotted line with one peak at 1.93s and subsequently falling to the level of background noise, but the *b4* high-point at 3.47s reaches this dynamic level in a very prominent *messa di voce,* indicated by the even rise to, and fall from, the peak. The sustained note from 4.78s lasts over 2 seconds before dying away over a further second to the end of the bar. Comparing this plot with the lower spectrogram in Figure 3, it can be seen that the *messa di voce* on the long $b4$ from 4.78s is achieved by colouring the spectrum of upper harmonic rather than varying the amplitude of the fundamental.

In contrast, no such articulations are apparent in KR, whether in the upper plot of Figure 3 or in the corresponding plot of Figure 5. The ornamental $b4$ at the start of the bar (c. 1.3s) is clearly shown to be played with almost as much weight as the peak at 3.23s, but, given the rapidly oscillating amplitude signal, it is difficult visually to pick out individual beats with security. Close-up examination of Figure 3 (not shown) reveals that the two peaks at 2.81s and 3.23s both belong to the third quaver of bar 1, so that the downbeat fourth quaver is attacked more weakly (c. 3.8s), though by a difference of only about 4dB. The peak at 5.03s likewise corresponds to a slight 'snatching' of the upbeat sixth quaver. In other words, this violinist sustains the tone throughout the phrase with little amplitude differentiation except for a slight 'snatch' of the upbeat quavers. In JEG, by contrast, the upbeat quavers are very lightly touched. We shall in due course read this effect in conjuction with our results on intonation, the strong $d5$ being the note that that was tuned some 19 cents flat.

As a final example of the power of frequency analysis, Figure 6 gives an image of pairs of frequencies close to *f#7*, which is the sixth harmonic of $b4$, and one of the harmonics exposed in Figure 4. The two frequencies have been chosen to allow a close view of the spread of vibrato displayed in Figure 4 (KR) and the characteristic 90 phasing of signal as the tone pans from one outer frequency band to the other. This produces the effect seen in Figure 6 where the peaks of the one frequency correspond to the troughs of the other. In the KR plot, this effect is most markedly evident in the region between the 6.11s and 7.27s markers, where the average cycle is 6.8cps between two sharp peaks, and 6.9cps between two sharp troughs. This exactly corresponds to the range we have already observed from other graphs. More interesting, here, however, is the comparative pattern in the lower plot. Here, the two frequencies tend to follow one another in phase, indicating that the variations in intensity or amplitude are not mirrored by frequency deviation. Given the closely parallel signals as amplitude fluctuates, it must be concluded that they each arise from the same instrument — the sustained tones of the accompanying strings could not be expected to match the rise and fall of the amplitude profile with such accuracy. The most probable explanation is therefore that the spectrogram is registering side-lobes (cf. Figure 2), that the parallel signals in adjacent frequency bands are an anomaly of the system.

We have shown how a visual image can be regarded as to some degree analogous to the aural image, and how it can help in quantifying certain properties of the performed music. Although a good ear will already have perceived far more detail than is possible to show on these graphs, certain details are revealed — for example, the flat tuning of the *d5* in KR and the emphasis in this recording on the third of each quaver-group, which an acute ear will capture but not perhaps with the confidence with which more prominent effects such as the sustained tone in KR, or the *messa di voce* in JEG, are perceived. All the same, it is not a frivolous question to ask whether these plots significantly inform a sensitive listening. May we be accused of falling into the positivist trap of prioritising the visual over the aural, of assuming that we must *see* an object before it can make an valid epistemological claim upon us? Does not performed music stand as a permanent testimony to the naivety of such assumptions? Why, we may ask, should we not trust our ears through listening instead of resorting to such elaborate lengths to formulate a visual analogue through quantisations that are merely approximate to the experience of listening and which, without due care, could give rise to false images of the sound-source?

It is certainly evident that much of what is shown by spectrographic analysis is little more than a visual analogue of what we have already recognised and perceived through listening. Nonetheless, acoustic analysis reinforces the experiential claims of the listening musician, namely that (1) performance can significantly determine the properties of the experience itself, and (2) the listening experience is not wholly private: hearing is not entirely 'subjective' in the sense of a strictly unverifiable or purely solipsistic mode of perception. It is apparent, too, that such analysis can serve to verify that what we think we are hearing is not illusory, a figment of the imagination, a check therefore on careless or prejudicial listening. Finally, acoustic analysis is a powerful medium for the education of the ear and as a diagnostic tool for the conscientious performer, the didactic possibilities of which have barely begun to be exploited.

III. THE LISTENING EXPERIENCE

PRESENCE, TRANSCENDENCE AND ILLUSION

The question remains, however: Where is the 'music'? If sounding music is constituted by the performer, what is the relationship between the morphology of the resulting sounds and the musical experience as constituted by the suitably equipped listener? If meanings are shifting and elusive, can acoustic analysis contribute meaningfully to such a discussion? At one level, it seems that musical meaning such as is constituted through performance may well be elusive, complex and multifaceted — Nicholas Cook shows in this volume that performed music is rarely the responsibility of only one single creative mind — yet, paradoxically, it also seems to be more direct, less culturally localised and less dependent upon the mediation of cognitive thought-processes, than is language. Surely there is a strong cognitive component in listening to music, but, as Anthony Pople points out, listeners are able to switch levels, at one moment listening *for* or *to* some property of the music, and at another 'merely' experiencing the music non-analytically.[50] Nicholas Cook writes that "listening to music for the purpose of establishing facts or formulating theories and listening to it for purposes of direct aesthetic gratification are two essentially different things". He goes on to claim that it is the condition in which one seems utterly to lose oneself in the experience of listening, which seems paradigmatically musical.[51] Indeed, one measure of an outstanding performance is surely the extent to

---

50. Anthony Pople, "Systems and Strategies: functions and limits of analysis", in: Anthony Pople (ed.), *Theory, Analysis and Meaning in Music.* Cambridge 1994, pp. 111–114.
51. Nicholas Cook, *Music, Imagination and Culture.* Oxford 1990, pp. 152 and 153. Cook coins the terms 'musicological' and 'musical' listening.

which it allows what I shall call 'transcendental listening', when we allow ourselves to loosen our customary experiential grip on the here-and-now *for the sake of* the music. Such transcendence seems neither escapist nor a denial of Self but rather a deepening of experience which, for T. S. Eliot, is a suitable simile of the transcendental properties of religious experience.[52]

The outstanding performance of a fine musical work is, I suggest, an invitation to transcendental listening in that, paradigmatically, it avoids drawing attention to itself *as* a performance (whether for positive or negative reasons). A distinction needs to be drawn, however, between the performer external to the music, and the performing persona, a term of considerable importance within the music itself. Wagner draws this distinction very sharply in his 1872 essay, *Über Schauspieler und Sänger*.[53] It is the second-rate 'comedian' who merely presents him- or herself, whereas the true performer becomes the focus of the artistic experience, the *persona* of the drama itself. Wagner even notes, with touching admiration, that his most admired singers such as Ludwig Schnor and Wilhelmine Devrient-Schröder were able to deceive even he, the composer, into losing consciousness of the origins of the music as work: the music becomes the singer. "There is one, and one only", Wagner writes, "to outvie the inspired mime [the actor or singer] in his self-offering: the author [composer] who *entirely forgets himself* in his joy at the mime's achievement."[54] Wagner further claims that the same applies to his orchestral musicians, his 'bandsmen'.[55] The point is essentially Proust's, as discussed in Section 1.[56] I do not claim this to be the only correct modality of listening, and grant that it may be more appropriate in a Wagner opera than a Bach Fugue. Nevertheless, Wagner's point that such performances

---

52. "You are the music while the music lasts (...)": *The Dry Salvages*, from: *The Four Quartets*. London 1944, p. 44. For discussion see Cook, *Music, Imagination and Culture*, p. 153.
53. Richard Wagner, "Actors and Singers", in: William Ashton Ellis (trans.), *Prose Works* Vol. 5, repr. 1995, p. 220. ("Über Schauspieler und Sänger", 1872).
54. Ibidem, p. 224.
55. Ibidem, p. 159.
56. See note 16.

and such listening experiences represent a merging of skills which is non-hierarchical surely reaches to the heart of the combined artistic enterprise which is composing, performing and listening to music.[57] Performance presence and the deictic role of the musical performer have as yet been little theorized,[58] far less the transcendental listening experience. What is already clear, however, is that the outstanding performance, as registered as listening experience, is the one that allows the listener to break the dichotomy imposed by consciousness between the 'I' and the 'Other', the critical, consciously cognitive faculty and the separateness of that which is being contemplated. The performance which leaves us thinking about questions of competence or value or authenticity — or even the work itself as something other, outside the present event — is the one which has failed to draw us, the listeners, into its own magical world. Or perhaps I should say, 'we' have failed, for transcendence requires two agencies, the transcended and the transcending: if I miss the experience, it may be through lack of concentration, external distractions or, importantly, inadequate preparation — to this extent, the cognitive and the transcendental modes of listening are not oppositional but dialectical.

Although transcendental listening is by all accounts a familiar experience for the music-lover, the notion of transcendence has been faired badly in both positivist and deconstructionist discourses over the last twenty years. For the logical positivist, transcendence strains the possibilities of verification: it is neither an object, a thing 'out there' to be subjected to examination, nor a particular 'state of consciousness' in so far as that might be examined in isolation from the encounter with the object, but a drawing together of the two. If, further, the experience is non-repeatable (since each new encounter with, say, the same recording implies a fresh conjunction of Self and Performance, just as each

---

57. Ibidem, p. 224.
58. For a structuralist, Greimasean account, see Eero Tarasti, *A Theory of Musical Semiotics*. Indiana 1994, pp. 98–114. For all his interest in the deicticity of performance, Tarasti does not escape the ideological bounds of *Werktreue* and hence fails to grasp the performer's primary function, to make musical sound.

new performance is a fresh conjunction of Work and Interpretation), we are dealing with something which is, to adopt a fashionable term from astronomy, a particularity. It therefore falls outside the ambit of logical positivism.[59]

Far more profound is Derrida's generalised critique of presence. It would take several volumes to do justice to Derrida's rich and varied arguments, as others better qualified than I have demonstrated.[60] Here, I propose to discuss one short passage from *Margins of Philosophy* in which J. L. Austin's study of spoken language, *How to do things with Words* is subjected to formal deconstruction.[61] Austin's text is itself of considerable interest to the musical performer, for it deals with 'performatives', the inflections which speaking imposes upon the written text.[62] A curious anomaly in Austin's book is his refusal to countenance the performatives of the actor, claiming that actors' enunciations are 'hollow or void' and hence that their use of language is 'parasitic' and cannot qualify as 'normal' use of language.[63] This point, incidentally, serves to emphasize an important difference between language and music, that in the latter there is no equivalent to 'normal' spoken language as distinct from 'performance': there are merely more or less formal performance contexts. In characteristic fashion, however, Derrida lights upon the opposition itself, shifting the focus onto the differentiation between 'parasitic' and 'normal' in language itself. If the former is marked as citation, as iteration of pre-conceived and intentional signs such as might be the task of the actor,

---

59. For a concise critical account, see Oswald Hanfling, *Logical Positivism*. Blackwell 1981.
60. From a vast literature, I recommend Andrew Bowie's books which demonstrate that Derridean critiques of logocentrism and presence are anticipated in the writings of the German Romantic poets and philosophers, Novalis in particular, and that solutions are there proposed that offer an escape from the closed set of aporias as formulated by Derrida. See especially *Aesthetics and Subjectivity from Kant to Nietzsche*. Manchester 1990, and *From Romanticism to Critical Theory: the Philosophy of German Literary Theory*. London 1997.
61. Jacques Derrida, *The Margins of Philosophy* (*Marges de la Philosophie*) (Alan Bass, trans.). London 1982; John L. Austin, *How to do things with Words*. Oxford 1962.
62. See also John R. Searle, *Speech Acts, an essay in the Philosophy of Language*. Cambridge 1969, p. 68.
63. Discussed in Derrida, *Margins*, p. 341.

the latter, according to Derrida, likewise cannot escape the anteriority of the sign. For example, while an actor who adopts a 'pathetic' tone is performing an iteration, literally so in so far as it will be a repeatable performance, a 'normal' speech-act will similarly access an already established set of conventional gestures and nuances in expressing an affect such as 'pathos'. Intention, to this extent, is itself citation. Thus, "the intention which animates utterance will never be completely present in itself and its content", where by 'present' Derrida seeks to invoke the full plenitude of the pre-constituted experiencing Self in the encounter with an equally explicit, given object.[64]

Derrida is aware that there are other perspectives, and deals with some of them in *Margins*. Again of interest to the performer is his analysis of Paul Valéry's accounts of voice and timbre in his *Cahiers*.[65] Valéry regarded timbre in spoken language as surpassing 'form and content': "as far as you are concerned, all I need do is watch you talk, listen to your timbre, the excitement in your voice (…). The content itself has no (…) essential property."[66] Derrida questions, however, whether timbre can lend itself to substitution, or whether it could be "a singular presence, the very upsurge [*sourdre*] of the source". His response is dogmatic: "I neither hear nor recognize the timbre of my voice (…) my style marks itself, it is only a surface that remains invisible and illegible for me". And so, the "spontaneous can emerge as the pure initiality of the event only on the condition that it does not itself *present itself*, on the condition of this inconceivable and *irrelevable* passivity in which nothing can present itself to itself". Leaving aside the subjective, empirical dimension that Derrida suddenly introduces here, it is evident that Derrida is willing to concede that "the value of the event is perhaps indissociable from that of presence" but insists that its value as event "remains rigorously incompatible with that of self-presence".[67]

---

64. Ibidem, p. 326.
65. "Qual Quelle: Valéry's Sources", in: *Margins*, pp. 275–299.
66. Derrida, *Margins*, p. 296.
67. Ibidem, pp. 296–297.

Derrida's critique of presence is therefore a critique of 'self-presence', not of the experience of presence, of what Derrida later calls its 'effect': "a general writing of which the system of speech, conciousness, meaning, presence, truth, etc., would only be an effect, to be analysed as such".[68] The effect of presence is real enough for Derrida, but what cannot be asserted is its claim to objectivity. But is it not a strictly positivist move to problematise effect on these grounds? If an effect is not to be trusted, if it has to be interrogated, analysed, and hence shown to be epistemologicall unreliable, does this not rebound upon epistemology itself for failing to account for the world as we experience it? Having rejected Husserlean phenomenology, Derrida seems to have no recourse except to fall back on positivist methods even while he deconstructs its discourse. No wonder he is so fascinated by the aporia. Derrida's warnings that we cannot make the leap from experience to verificationists' concepts of truth are well made, but his deconstruction of experience and presence turns out to be merely a deconstruction of the positivist insistence that these be verifiable. As musicians, we know that, even though our experiences of composing, performing and listening to music are 'merely' cultural constructs, they are no less meaningful to us as living, thinking and experiencing human beings.

Why, then, do we have to reduce the art-work to that which it is not? In his great posthumous study, *Aesthetic Theory*, Adorno had already by-passed post-structuralist critiques of presence in relation to the art-work by claiming that art *is* illusory, and necessarily so: "The seal of authentic artworks is that what they appear to be appears as if it could not be prevaricated, even though discursive judgement is unable to define it."[69] In these terms, in so far as performances are perceived as 'definitive', they expose their illusory character of seeming to be that which they cannot be. The performer's ideal might thus be expressed in terms of creating a

---

68. Ibidem, p. 329.
69. Theodor Adorno, *Aesthetic Theory*, p. 132 (AT p. 199). I subsequently refer to the English translation as H-K and the original as AT. For a lucid discussion see Simon Jarvis, *Adorno, a critical introduction*. Oxford 1998, p. 115.

performance sufficiently convincing that the listener is deceived into judging it definitive, while knowing it is not. One of the several reasons Adorno puts forward is that, were the art-work to assume a positivist objectivity, it could make no claim to being other than a mere object in the world. The *objet trouvé*, in being already 'found', is no longer merely an object, as Heidegger had argued in *Der Ursprung des Kunstwerkes*.[70] Adorno's central point is that as soon as we perceive something *as* art, its relationship to the world, its own origins and its meanings are all instantly problematised. In Derrida's terms this art-property would be an 'effect', yet Adorno claims that it is for that reason that it is able to exert its unique magic, in a modality different from the elegant mathetical formula or chess solution (which are arguably aesthetic) for being inherently enigmatic (*rätselhaft*).[71] The music that holds no secrets, or the performance that offers no surprises (where the most subtle are often the most effective), is as dead as a dead metaphor. It is still music, but it fails to pass the experiential test of artistry precisely in failing as 'effect', as at once compelling, mysterious, and in some enigmatic way, meaningful.

Behind Adorno's thesis is the assumption, or perhaps the corollary, that the human spirit thirsts for the enigmatic, that art's *Rätselcharakter* captures something that has special meaning for us. I would like to suggest that the key to this enigma lies in the 'effect' of experience or presence which is itself inherently problematic for the human condition, caught as it is between its physical presence in and of the world and its disposition to conscious self-reflection as the origin of the effect of transcendence. However, transcendence is not a denial of the world but a moving *through* the medium to some imaginary other; to this extent, the experience of listening to music is likewise dependent upon the morphology of the sounds perceived. Analysis thus comes into play as a technique of informing the nature of that experience,

---

70. "The Origin of the Work of Art", in: Martin Heidegger, *Basic Writings* (David Farrell Krell, trans.). London 1978, p. 139-211.
71. "Ultimately art-works are enigmas in terms not of their composition but of their truth content": H-K p. 127, AT p. 192.

even though analysis alone could never capture that experience in its plenitude as constitutive of art. Analysis should therefore seek to expose aporias in the art-work as well as whatever there is of the closed, logical formulation. Joyce's *Ulysses* fascinates not because it is logically closed but because it plays upon a kaleidoscopic sequence of open events and human situations. Adorno suggests that every art-work partakes to some degree in this resistance to rigid formulation, that it is inherently enigmatic.

EXPERIENCE AND SEMIOTICS

I have argued that poststructuralist critiques of presence cannot be sustained in the presence of the art-work. The art-work is, by definition, an effect, an illusion, albeit one that is profoundly important for us as thinking and experiencing human beings. To this extent a good performance is itself an art-work, as Kivy proclaimed, for it too is illusory, both in the ways Adorno catalogues for the art-work itself, and when it asserts, illicitly but effectively, its authenticity as the definitive performance. The other side of Adorno's dialectic, however, is that the art-work comprises material, *Stoff*, that determines its property of appearance (*Schein*).[72] Performance of course depends upon this property, which is one reason by which it has been marginalized in positivist musicological discourse. Yet it is at this level that analysis comes into play, not to explain the work, but to demonstrate certain discernible properties that are salient within it. This is the method proposed by the late Naomi Cumming in a remarkable study of "Erbarme dich" recently published in *Music Analysis*.[73]

Cumming begins by asking why it is that "Erbarme dich" always exerts such a powerful affective response for her. She seeks to situate her personalised affective response firmly within the score-content itself, a structuralist method which presupposes that her

---

72. H-K pp. 100ff, AT pp. 154ff. Adorno did not make the connection between art and performance in his theory of art. His comments on performance in AT are surprisingly unfocussed and distinctly casual.
73. Naomi Cumming, "The Subjectivities of 'Erbarme dich'", in: *Music Analysis* 16/1 (March 1997), p. 5.

response is a culturally mediated 'given' and hence available to us all. She seeks, however, to transcend structuralism by presenting analogues between content and experience, a move that leads her to engage directly with the problem of subjectivity. Drawing on Pierce, Merleau-Ponty, Gadamer and from unpublished work by David Lidov, Cumming argues that, while the action of experiencing is that of a constituted subject, that subject is itself constituted by the experience: "'[i]ndividuality' or 'the subject' does not exist first in order to originate actions, but is formed by actions and evident in them."[74] Subjectivity itself then becomes a cultural phenomenon. From this vantage-point she is able to contemplate the expressive properties of Bach's aria not as correlates of pre-existent terms in the experiencing subject, but rather as themselves constituting the subject: "Instead of viewing the subject as a bundle of static subjective states that exist to be 'expressed', we should look to acts of expression as forming the subject and constituting his or her states, through a unique combination of elements."[75] This is a characteristically Deweyean theme: we do not have to deny experience in the contemplation of the art work but should seek, rather, to understand the work as a medium of interaction between Self and the particular world it seems to present to us. In *Art as Experience*, Dewey defines experience as "the result, the sign, and the reward of that interaction of organism and environment which, when it is carried to the full, is a transformation of interaction into participation and communication".[76]

Dewey radically rejects the traditional metaphysical dualisms of subject and object, mind and matter, a mark he says of 'contraction and withdrawal'. It is art, he says, that stands as "the living and concrete proof that man is capable of restoring consciously, and thus on the plane of meaning, the union of sense, need, impulse and action characteristic of the live creature".[77] This somewhat heady proposition captures something of the hubris of

---

74. Ibidem, p. 16.
75. loc.cit.
76. John Dewey, *Art as Experience*. New York 1934, p. 22.
77. Ibidem, p. 25.

performance itself, the ideal of achieving a union of sense, need, impulse and action, 'on the plane of meaning'. But it also characterises the activity of listening. Dewey stressed that listening is no passive reception of a given message but an action, a motivated constitution of meaning, an experiencing of the sounds we hear. Consonant with post-structuralist theory, he shows that there is no 'innocent ear', for present experience is always already mediated by past experience: to this extent, experience is an activity mediated by intersubjective consensus, a process that ultimately constitutes culture. And so the semiotic, the intersubjective 'plane of meaning', is dependent upon experience itself but also contributes symbiotically to its constitution in the act of listening.

Yet experience is not neutral or transparent: the experience of hearing "Erbarme dich" cannot be confused with that of hearing the preceding recitative, Bach's extraordinary evocation of Peter's denial. Thus, inevitably, we turn back to semiotics. Following Pierce, Cumming notes the subjective location of the interpretant, that which authorizes the association between signifier and signified as 'mental investment', yet notes also that signs cannot be 'private mental items'.[78] That is to say, if we hear a violin vibrato as a sign of 'vocality' (her example), we establish an association dependent upon a specific and publically available interpretant. Participation, for example in the Baroque Affects, is not "indulging in an arbitrary whim, but engaging personally with a shared experience and allowing it to become individualised".[79] Neither is such an experience affectively neutral: "hearing a warm voice, dejected gesture and suppressed volition are each acts of interpretation in which the listener's mental involvement is implied, without suggesting a purely private realm of activity".[80] Cumming thus leaves her readers in no doubt that her affective response to Bach's aria is, or could be, our response.

---

78. Cumming, "Subjectivities", p. 15.
79. Ibidem, p. 7.
80. Ibidem, p. 17.

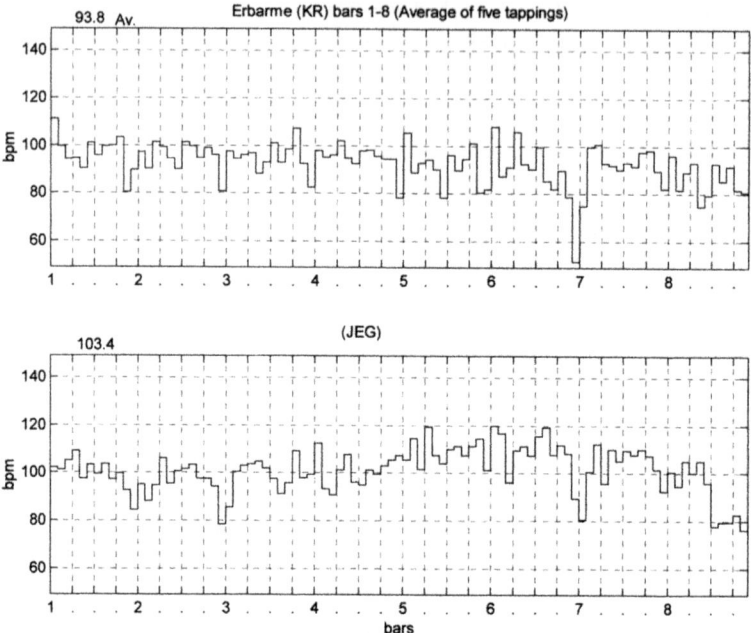

Figure 7: "Erbarme dich", bars 1-8: Variation of beat-length by tapping (average of five attempts). Beats-per-minute plotted for each beat. Three quavers per vertical grid-line.

Cumming offers the analyst an excellent model of discourse that does not deny the givenness of the score nor the reality of the listening experience. And yet, for all its dependence upon contemporary hermeneutic theory, Cumming's account is flawed in so far as it fails to acknowledge the mediacy and immediacy of performance in the listening experience. To this extent she falls into the familiar musicologist's trap of assuming that one can read *directly* from score to the listening experience without acknowledging performances and performance traditions. Analysis, if an inevitable fall from this union of Self and Other empowered by performed music, can nonetheless engage with performed music at this level, as well as at the level of score-analysis. It thus has a role to play in marking and deepening the listener's cognitive encounters with the music without which participation, *methexis*, cannot occur. I propose to close by reviewing my acoustic analyses of KR and JEG in the light of Cumming's discussion of subjectivities and Adorno's remarkable discussion of art as enigma. It will be interesting to gauge the extent to which the two performances are able

performance and the listening experience

to offer divergent experiences, and the extent to which acoustic analysis is able to reveal such enigmatic properties as can be ascribed to the performance. It should already be clear that the analysed properties of the sound itself are objective (provided we hear them at all), but my reading of them will be strictly hermeneutic, an act of interpretation always focused on the experience of listening.

INTERPRETING PERFORMANCE

I begin with a few words on tempo, an aspect of performance we avoided in Section 2. José Bowen's study of rhythm demonstrates that three levels need to be considered, the overall or average tempo and its proportionality to sections in other tempos, the 'phrase tempo', such as might vary from one phrase to the next, and 'flexibility' within the phrases or bars. Figure 7 shows a comparison between successive beats in KR and JEG, made by the tapping method upon which contemporary performance-analysis has largely depended.[81] KR is about 10bpm (quaver beats-per-minute) slower than JEG, but more interesting is the greater variability in JEG at both phrase level and beat-by-beat flexibility. The second phrase in JEG is marked by a new average tempo (bars 5-7), itself some 10bpm faster than the opening tempo of c. 100bpm; KR in bars 5-7 shows greater variation than in the opening bars but no overall change of tempo. At the level of flexibility, it is interesting in KR that there is a definite tenuto in the final one or two beats of every bar, of the order of some 15 bpm; the tempo is always regained on each down-beat. In bars 5-7, this occurs also at the

---

81. The method involves the operator tapping the keyboard for each beat or bar, the recorded timings then being accessible for plotting and analysis. The question of precision of this method has not been seriously broached in the literature. The software normally depends upon the computer's internal clock which is refreshed at irregular times of the order of 50ms (0.05s), i.e. above the limen of difference perception. Recent research on the physiology of tapping shows a gap between sound-generation and the tap-event of the order of c. 30ms, a remarkable correlation between human muscular and aural skills (Geoffrey Walsh and Peter Johnson, in preparation). This however gives a maximum margin of error of < 0.1s for each tap, but since each error is compensated by the next, errors are non-cumulative. See Bowen, "Tempo, Duration and Flexibility", p. 130. Figure 7 shows the average results of five 'tappings' for each recording.

half-bar, the first beats of each group of three quavers being markedly faster in bar 6, and tending to be faster throughout. In JEG, the flexibility is less predictable. Tenutos on the final quaver beat of bars 2 and 3 contrast with marked accelerandos at the end of bars 4-5. Similarly, some of the down-beats are faster, some slower than the surrounding beats. In both recordings, there is a marked articulation of the start of bar 7 (very extreme in KR) and correspondingly little emphasis for the start of bar 8.

In summary, KR is predictable in its use of flexibility, reducing the semantic content of tempo-variation to the syntactical level of articulating down-beats and phrase divisions. In JEG, there is, rather, a counterpoint between syntax and tempo flexibility. The effect is dynamic, the kinaesthetic sweep of Bach's lines marked by rubato at bar and phrase levels.

Also potentially kinaesthetic are Bach's notated on-the-beat ornaments. In JEG, they give a spring-board effect, as is suggested by the amplitude relationship between the several b_4s and the d_5 in Figure 5. This lightness is reinforced by a graceful double-dotting so that the final semiquaver of the dotted figure is both short and very light. From Figure 5, we can trace the kinaesthetic properties of the lightly touched down-beat slide at the beginning of bar 1, the strong but brief d_5, the short semiquaver and the shorter third quaver beat defined by the *pizzicato* cello as 2.82s, the strong fourth quaver and again the lighter 6th quaver at 4.2s. The relatively gentle gradients up to the peaks are also perceptually significant: the amplitude rise is in the order of 6dB, and on-set times in the order of 0.3s for the longer durations. A conductor might vocalise this 'bouncing' rhythm (from the violin's first upbeat) as: 'di, diiah--di-di, diiah--di-di, diiah——'. The spectrogram in Figure 3 shows the peaks ('-ah') to be articulated by the characteristic opening and closing of the upper harmonic spectrum we have identified with the *messa di voce*. By contrast, KR shows none of these traits. At the start of b.1 the rising minor sixth $f\#$ - d is interrupted rather than facilitated by the heavy b_4 at the start of the slide (Figure 5, upper plot, 1.4s). In kinaesthetic terms, the lift to d_5 then requires effort, a sequential 'climbing' rather than a front-loaded 'springing'. This heaviness is emphasized in the flat tuning of the d_5, as if the opening minor sixth were difficult to achieve, and by the lengthening durations of the first three quaver beats (Figure 7). That these effects are contained within a pervasive legato illustrates a level of withdrawal of deictic presence from the solo violin, its singing line a little tentative against the prominent accompaniment.

None of these properties of KR are indicative of poor performance, for the Richter recording is justly honoured as one of the finest mainstream performances on record. To my mind, this performance is nonetheless problematic precisely because there is such a close congruence between its several explicit signifiers and the aria in Bach's composition. All the signifiers, metaphorically speaking, are 'down', catching an explicit property of the text and the present moment of the narrative. And yet, ironically, it is precisely in this close correlation between the signifiers of the performed music and the narrative that the performance loses its potency, just as it is the conjunction of the lightness of a dance with the prayer for forgiveness that lends to JEG — and, authenticists may claim, the 'music itself' — that subtlety which rests upon the enigmatic. It is at this level that Naomi Cumming's excellent account of the "Subjectivities of 'Erbarme dich'" is ultimately disappointing. She notes the subtlety of 'affective complexity' and the 'distantiation' provided by the 'framing' of the music in the more or less conventional 'stabilizing framework' suggesting "an effective containment that it cannot itself fulfil";[82] nonetheless, an entire dimension of the music's semiotic potentiality is ignored, namely the element of dance. Thus she can remark that "playing too fast will (…) trivialise its affective intensity, suggesting an unwarranted superficiality of character as the content of the gestures is sacrificed to the continuity of the phrase".[83] Of course this may be the case, particularly for a given type of audience, but the point is meaningless without reference to specific examples. Figure 7 shows that JEG's faster tempo is

---

82. Cumming, "Subjectivities", pp. 34–35.
83. Ibidem, p. 31.

associated with greater differentiation of gestural content than is KR's slower tempo.

In fact, Cumming's remarks about what she took to be the aria itself relate only to a particular performing tradition exemplified by KR; indeed, this is the one recording she mentions by name. The opening violin solo of "Erbarme dich" was, for Cumming, 'vocal', which, as we have observed in discussing Figures 3 and 6 in particular, is consistent with KR's sustained, legato style. The wide jagged lines in the plotting of the *b4* frequency-band in Figure 5 indicate regular variation of frequency consistent with vibrato, but also the sustained dynamic over several seconds. This playing, as Cumming points out, closely matches the vocal soloist's sustained vocal line (Janet Baker in KR). But an intentionally authentic performance such as JEG generates other codes: the period instrument violin creates a line that is not a 'vocalise', at least not according to later twentieth century connotations of the term, but presents, rather, a dancing persona, weaving ceremonially, reverentially yet still evocatively around the more static lines of Michael Chance's limpid countertenor voice. The listener is therefore offered a highly complex synthesis: those highly emotive words, "Herz und Auge weint vor Dir bitterlich", intoned with a remarkable purity of tone, supported by the extraordinary tapestry of Bach's counterpoint and accompanying textures, and a solo violin (which, we are mildly reminded, is elsewhere the instrument of the Devil himself), weaving a gentle, light-footed yet not irreverent *pastorale*, matching purity of singing voice with purity of gestural movement. Is this not to conjure rich allusions, powerful enough already to transcend the earth-boundedness of meaning? Is it not a mystery intoned, one in which we, the listeners, may yet participate but not fully comprehend?

We do not need to ask whether Bach intended this music to be performed in the manner of the *pastorale*, but we can confidently assert that the embodiment of this property in JEG conjures for the contemporary listener allusions which are all the more intriguing for being enigmatic. How can the abject, penitential Soul, seeking forgiveness of its Lord whom it has personally betrayed, at the same time, *dance* to a pastoral 12/8, complete with drones elevated to the full string orchestra and subtly articulated by unmistakably dancing dotted rhythms? This enigma, I suggest, helps to explain why the object we are dealing with is art and not religious discourse or polemic. It reminds us of those magical major-key portrayals of grief such as Orpheus's *Che farò senz' Euridice,* or the opening of Stravinsky's *Orpheus* in which a balletic portrayal of Orpheus's loss of Euridice is offered with cool, neutral music that abjures any reference to standard tropes of grief yet, for all that — or, perhaps, because of it — can be very moving.

By appearing merely to present the score-content, KR nonetheless makes its own powerful commentary upon it. Firstly, there is the performance *topos* of 'reverence', one which perhaps dominates mainstream performance practice of Bach in the mid-to-late twentieth century. The signifiers are, I suggest, widely recognised: the even lines, the relatively thick textures, the slowish tempos and the tendency to maintain a steady unvarying tempo — all this, together with a general heaviness of rhythmic articulation lending to the music an air of sobriety and, surely, of authority. Secondly, and perhaps consequently, there is the refusal to respond to the kinaestheic allusions of Bach's dotted 12/8 rhythm: KR's performance might suitably be notated in a moderato 3/4. Behind this conjunction in KR is an implicit distrust of the physical and sensual, a bequest to Christianity from Plato and St. Paul that has found fertile ground in the academicism both of mid-twentieth century musicology and performance practice, of which Karl Richter is an authoritative and justly admired exponent. To this extent, JEG represents a more liberal melding of sacred and secular connotations. If, following Richard Taruskin, period instrument performance is 'our music', the way we want to hear it today, JEG marks the rediscovery in later 20th century Bach performance practice of the physical, the kinaesthetic, not (here) as licentiousness but as a medium through which even a Passion can find new (or old) meanings and hence can be experienced in ways unimagined by the mid-century mainstream performer or score-reader. It is surely no accident that this new tradition of period instrument performance-practice is coincident with the historical moment of the rediscovery in philosophy of the body. Merleau Ponty, Mark Johnson, David Lidov and a host of younger scholars are finding in a philosophy of the body certain solutions to the problems inherent in Platonic idealism and the Cartesian dichotomies, problems rehearsed but not resolved in post-stucturalist discourse.[84] In an important new book, John Shepherd and Peter Wicke pursue the physical 'connectedness' of music, not by claiming for music the status of the 'pre-linguistic', 'pre-symbolic', 'pre-rational' and 'pre-logical', as do Lacanian writers such as Julia Kristeva, neither as a modalisation specifically of the unconscious, but as a sophisticated means of articulating consciousness in and through its physical being as a parallel and complementary mode to language.[85]

This of course problematises critical discourse itself. Carolyn Abbate writes in the Preface to *Unsung Voices* that "interpreting music involves a terrible and unsafe leap between object and exegesis, from sound that seems to signify nothing (and is nonetheless splendid) to words that claim discursive sense but are, by comparison, modest and often unlovely".[86] Yet sound does not "seem to signify nothing". Musical sound is replete with meaning, albeit primarily 'soundly' in its modality.[87] And, for all the problems and the ultimate futility in seeking to capture the musical experience in words, it is evident that composers, performers and their critics have evolved over the centuries forms of verbal and symbolic coding by which to capture certain salient properties of this meaning, hence the stock of generalised 'expressive terms' and *topoi* known to every composer and appropriately prepared performers and listeners. Whether, as Nicholas Cook argues in this volume, words constitute the experience of music itself, or

---

84. See especially Mark Johnson, *The Body in the Mind: the Bodily Basis of Meaning, Imagination, and Reason.* Chicago 1987.
85. John Shepherd and Peter Wicke, *Music and Cultural Theory.* London 1997.
86. Carolyn Abbate, *Unsung Voices: Opera and Musical Narrative in the Nineteenth Century.* Princeton 1991, p. xv.
87. Susanne Langer's chapter "On Significance in Music", in: *Philosophy in a New Key.* Harvard 1942, pp. 204–245 has much yet to offer in the reevaluation of music's connectedness.

whether they are necessarily subservient to the ontologically prior musical experience, they certainly play an essential functional role alongside music notation in the arts of composition, performance, listening and criticism. In this paper, I have tried to show that acoustic analysis can play a complementary role. Analysis can perhaps make good some of the limitations of language in capturing properties of the musical as it emerges through performance and upon which the transcendence of the deep listening experience depends. But I have also argued that such an investment in the demonstrable can only inform, qualify, point towards that which we need already to have experienced. That experience, as a property of the genuinely artistic, is ultimately enigmatic, from which it follows that the analytical enterprise, for all its usefulness, always risks destroying that which it seeks to value in attempting fully to encompass and define it. Knowledge is power, but art, and in particular music-in-performance, offers men and women a different, deeper relationship between themselves and their worlds.

A ROADMAP FOR ORPHEUS?

ABOUT NON-LINEAR CODES OF MUSIC FOR THE DESCENT INTO ITS UNDERWORLD

Hans Zender

PART I

Our theoretical understanding of music, the way we handle it in practice, and our compositional *poiesis* are to a great extent based on a series of tacit assumptions whose implications and significance are never stated. Even the classical avant-garde, i.e. the 2nd Viennese school and the serial composition technique that followed are no exception; on the contrary: both seem to cling to these axioms that promise logical consistency.

The fact that music should be a finite, coherent entity where all individual elements are related to one another and put into a hierarchical perspective, somehow seems to require no justification. The tacit agreement that sound sources should be compact, i.e. be used in concentrated form in the smallest space possible, is taken for granted, to the same extent that a cinema screen or the canvas of a painting are limited surfaces. The fact that our tonal structures should be based on the equidistant system of equal temperament, while our rhythmic structures rely on a system whereby time is divided into equal units, has hardly ever once been questioned since the classical period. A work written today is expected to be different from music written during earlier periods, and to use a different set of symbols and other stylistic means. The author must beware of using a language too close to the tone of voice used by other authors. Music has come to be taken for the creation of individuals; the outside world is expected to stick to its role of performer ('interpreters') or passive listener. The work of art is seen as identical to itself, i.e. a stable and coherent mental entity no longer subject to time-based transformations or evolution: philosophers would call it an idea, scientists and technicians would refer to it as an object.

It is precisely this idea that cannot, in all earnest, be upheld at a time when the experience of history and the exploration of alien cultures play such a predominant role. The fact that the distance of time and space as well as cultures simply demand an interpretation, and therefore, albeit it willy-nilly, also a transposition can no longer be denied. Even recording something in writing "includes (…) some form of translation" says Kuno Lorenz in the introductory chapter to his work *Indische Denker*. A musical work cannot be understood simply based on its score; the symbols on the score are all related to a future 'actualisation' by means of a performance, with every performance being a new interpretation of these symbols and therefore a different version of the piece. The score itself is already an interpretation: it translates the composer's innermost thoughts into the symbol set of a given period. A work cannot be fully understood without hints to its receptional history — and the latter starts during the creation of the text.

Works of art have no stable identity: they are 'living' creatures and thus also subject to the dynamic energies of time. The quest of history-oriented musicians for the 'one and only' reproduction of old music is quixotic at best. Yet, even contemporary composers should beware of being lured into using an ever more precise notation of their works — that may stretch as far as video-taping a so-called 'authorised' performance. Even disregarding the fact that such a recording would also be subject to interpretation, taping one performance would merely be a vain attempt to suppress other possible readings of a work.

Having adopted this non-linear openness for the future inherent to any written record, a second stage will be to recognise the author as a human being who, through his of her new inventions, also produces new interpretations of historic forms, whether he or she is aware of this or not. Even by disregarding links to any aesthetic interpretation (which is almost impossible), his or her symbols are still related to conventions through their negation. The author simply cannot deny being engaged in an on-going dialogue with history.

For the same reason, he or she can no longer use certain conventions, such as equal temperament or metre 'based on the metronome' without first questioning them. He or she knows that there are alternatives and that there always have been. He or she must therefore understand that simply conforming to conventions is already an artistic decision.

This is also true of the fundamental question whether an artistic form must present itself as a unity. No other 'axiomatic' premise goes straight to the root of the specifically European understanding of our culture like this one; those who deny this question state the possibility of the existence of works of art devoid of any organisational principle that links the beginning to the end, and therefore, that logical consistency is not part of the constituting characteristics of artistic shaping.

20th-Century music is characterised by, on the one hand, the severest systematic formal construction principles ever, and on the other hand — Surrealism is only the most striking example — by its access to the pre-logic area of unstructured artistic activity, where, at best, the nuclei of systematic approaches of more conscious stages are to be found. Dealing with this pre-logic area in an artistic — and thus aesthetically justified — way is no longer possible with familiar linear strategies that allowed us to structure our sonic and rhythmic fields. One cannot apply linear techniques to the area of non-linearity.

Art not only reflects the evolution of social structures but also the evolution of conscience. Modern-day artists are forced to deal with problems that artists of previous centuries were unaware of. While conscience of form of 'classical' artists was considered to be the awareness of an autonomous, coherent 'I', non-linear — informal, anti-aesthetic, pluralistic — aspects of contemporary art tend to expand the 'I', to explode it, to transcend it, while seeing it in its conditionality. It goes without saying that reason and traditional logic only play a minor part in this, even though the conscious 'I' must remain intact during these inexplicable activities. Who else could indeed see to it that such currents do not lead to a regression of conscience into pre-individuality or the archaic, but rather to an 'increased' awareness?

This is precisely where the weaknesses of several musical currents that venture into the non-linear become apparent — regardless of whether these currents focus on the dissolution of a unifying structure, the conquest of decentralised space, new harmonic and rhythmic concepts, or a mix of these tendencies. For example: a composer who inserts random techniques into linearly proportional time units with a view to creating an experience of the relativity of time in a non-classically defined exchange, produces an ambiguous, half-hearted time frame. If his or her collages or style constructions treat music from different periods as equal 'musical material', he or she fails to notice that the same two minutes of time are not used in the same way by Machaut, Bach, Wagner, or Schönberg. By merely changing the 'classic' seating order of orchestras so as to have the musicians surround the audience in various patterns, he or she sacrifices the possibilities of making space experienceable in its musically virtually unexplored capacity as enabler and destroyer of musical structures for a merely nice effect at best.

The question then is how the artist can take the necessary decisions for handling these non-linear powers. John Cage seems to have found a solution by leaving control to coincidence. But this is merely exorcising the devil with Beelzebub: rational strategies are replaced by statistic procedures that are merely a different kind of formal control, where the 'I' no longer decides. The feeling, sensible, 'I' must take part in this process, however, even if it realises that it alone will not be able to finish the artistic process. The 'I' must therefore team up with its 'Non-I' — the subconscious — in a new, much profounder, sense than in old art, where intuition, inspiration, and 'moods' have, of course, always been used. When it comes to non-linear procedures, it is precisely these formal decisions, which used to be imposed by the aesthetic prerogatives of the day, that now need to be set free through a *tour de force*, triggered by the composer's vitality. How long can a citation last? How profound should a chaotic complex be? To what extent should unity prevail over diversity? For these decisions, the composer at his or her desk needs physical and psychic tension, comparable to the tension the performing artist needs on stage, in order to turn the 'symbolic activities' into a living power that can be experienced by the listener. Morton Feldman once described his act of composing as a kind of performance that could only last for so long — which is the exact opposite of a calculated approach. And yet, these procedures will never relieve us from the necessity to organise our symbols into the clearest set possible and to establish a hierarchical relationship among them. Failure to do so will lead to the result of our work being a senseless juxtaposition of individual moments. Composing today must be an individual mix of rational methods for controlling linear time-based processes and intuitive decisions about non-linear aspects. It should be noted, however, that these decisions need not be found in a kind of dream conscience, as the cliché of romantic artists would have us believe, but can be the result of active conscious acts possibly supported by concentrational methods. In an act of 'self test', every composer needs to find his or her ideal mix. Composing is self-experience, or as the philosopher Heraclitus put it: "I explored myself":

Ἐδιζησάμην ἐμεωυτόν

PART II

No composer, when asked about his or her technique, can declare it to be generally mandatory. Much rather, he or she behaves in the way the oracle is related to Delphi, about which Heraclitus said: "The master of the oracle neither says something nor hides something; he hints":

ὁ ἄναξ, οὗ τὸ μαντεῖόν ἐστι τὸ ἐν Δελφοῖς, οὔτε λέγει οὔτε κρύπτει ἀλλὰ σημαίνει.

In the same way, a composer speaking about his work experience can, at best, provide hints for others; this is the only form of authenticity we may claim, and that shall be the aim of the following discussion of the mix of linear and non-linear procedures in three of my works.

I. STEPHEN CLIMAX

The opera I wrote in the early eighties, *Stephen Climax*, consists of two lyrically and musically autonomous and therefore independent layers that sometimes sound simultaneously, sometimes in a juxtaposition identified by means of clear cuts. For the lyrics of the 'Brothel Chapter' taken from James Joyce's *Ulysses* (in the excellent translation by Wollschläger), I invented a music with numerous stylistic elements that one could call 'chimerical' because it not only quotes characteristic examples of the treasure of the last 1000 years of European music but also transforms them using specific compositional techniques, thus turning them into ambiguous entities. For the scenes of the stylite Simeon (whose story I discovered in Hugo Ball's *Byzantine Christianity*), I wrote strictly unified serial music reminiscent of classical Modernism that, by its ascetic and constructionist nature, is clearly different from the swampy districts of the anti-opera.

It should be noted that the historic material is always related to individual characters of the piece, as is the use of certain intervals. Thus, the character of Stephen is represented by means of a fourth as well as late Middle-Age music (where the fourth plays a predominant part). The round, soft character of Leopold Bloom is represented by means of a major third and baroque music. In the same way that Bloom sees the apparition of his grand-father, who is represented by a chimerically transformed cantata by Bach (*Amore traditore*), the character of the prophet Elijah befalls Stephen to the sound of an (anonymous) Sanctus from the 14th Century. The third protagonist, Lynch, loves Renaissance and augmented seconds. Lynch keeps dreaming of himself as a Renaissance nobleman until Cesare Borgia (now an inhabitant of hell) appears to the music of Monteverdi and Byrd. The ladies of the brothel dance to the sounds of parodied salon music of the 19th Century, while the aura of Stephen's dead mother consists of narrow quarter-tone intervals.

The stroll through European musical history that emerges from this juxtaposition (the "cat's stroll through the mud" as one of the ladies says) is not structured in the way Joyce uses this stylistic element (in the doctor's chapter of his novel with the stroll through several stages of the English language), i.e. in a linear fashion. Much rather, the music seems to jump to and fro among various periods, and confronts these diverging stylistic elements with the 'pure white' of the Simeon music during the work. All distorting manipulations applied to the historic material keep using the stylite's 'series' for embodying the 'chimeras', which is true both of the pitches and note duration. This represents the culmination of absurdity because the serial technique is not compatible with the tonal and metric structure of the old works being quoted. It is precisely this absurd, 'wrong', compositional behaviour that triggers something very rare in contemporary music, namely comic elements — more specifically structural comic elements that have a stronger impact than punctual comic effects. Time and again, the real theme of the opera becomes apparent in those moments of friction of two colliding stylistic worlds: the absurd situation that arises when symbols of a particular meaning system collide with other systems and suddenly lose or change their sense. Because we witness how, after a short transition through a chaotic and illegible zone (a 'crisis of meaning') these symbols organise themselves into a new aesthetic significance — a non-linear process that cannot be captured by traditional compositional logic. Already in 1969, Roland Barthes, in his structural analyses, talked about the 'non-linear codes' of literature.

2. MUJI NO KYÔ

While *Stephen Climax* as well as several others of my works (*Dialog mit Haydn, Hölderlin lesen I, "Winterreise", Schumann-Phantasie*) are based on the non-linear 'history' code, my 'Asian' works deal with the more fundamental problem of differing 'valence' of certain musical time structures. Each musical structure imposes a characteristic shape onto (meaninglessly flowing) natural time. The infinite variety of these characters can be assigned to two poles: they either tend towards an absolutely uniform music that materialises through endless repetitions and symmetrical organisation, or towards its opposite, a totally asymmetrical sequence of completely different shapes; the time structure is either centrifugal or centripetal.

The listener is used to conforming to a certain type of time structure within a work, whether this is the purposeful dynamics of the Beethoven tradition or the deconstructing entropic character of a work of the American school that seems to reverse the time axis; or the static of a fugue by Bach that shows the same on ever-changing levels; or fragmentary fractional structures. In many of my 'Asian' pieces, I have attempted to bring such diverging time directions together in the context of the work.

Muji no kyô consists of 18 parts of more or less equal length that are organised in an A-B-A-B-... sequence, where the A and B parts are so utterly different that they never meet or mediate but appear as totally different bodies. While the A parts consist of a series of 12 micro structures with different characteristics that bear no relation to one another, let alone present identical segments, each B part, during its duration, repeats one single musical shape in quasi endless, free ensemble playing by the musicians involved. On the one hand, there is the completely asymmetrical, 'open' time structure (extremely centrifugal), and on the other hand, time turned sound, static, 'image'. Through the regular alternation of the two time types, the listener is gradually prepared to 'simultaneously' dwell in two different perceptions of time; at the end of the piece, these two formal types are superimposed in the listener's memory — even though the piece itself contains not a single layer of these two time structures.

In *Furin no kyo*, I used a similar system for combining five different types of musical time shapes; other possibilities are being explored in my *Lo Shu*-series.

3. SHIR HASHIRIM

This work, a *Canto* that lasts two hours and fifteen minutes, contains a number of relevant elements for our subject. The first is related to the time structure. Here, the 'achievement of the impossible' has been attempted, both in the relationship between micro structure and macro structure, and the question of 'centrifugal' and 'centripetal time structure'. The underlying thought was that of self-similarity (analogy): what happens on the microscopic level must also work on the macroscopic level; either should contain a time structure whose centrifugal or centripetal energies balance one another.

In order to achieve this paradox, a series of numbers was selected supposed to symbolise the progress of musical time both on the microscopic and macroscopic level:

1	2	3	4	5	6	7	8	9	10	11	12	13	14	15	16	17
1		2		3		4		5		6		7		8		9
1				2				3				4				5
1								2								3
1																2

Each number symbolises an individual musical '*Gestalt*'. The top row simply means that new musical shapes are being introduced until the end of the piece. The rows below it symbolise the 'memory' of form: by repeating shapes that have already been played, the listener is reminded of them at regular intervals, from short intervals (symbolising 'short-term memory') to increasingly longer ones. (During the compositional process, the repeated shapes can be read before or after the shapes in the top row, or even at the same time.) At the end of the symbolised sequence of shapes, only the first half of the shapes in the top row will have appeared twice or three times, while the second half is sounded only once: a 'mean' so to speak between open and closed form.

This 'formal key' is then applied to all time units of the work. Let us first look at the central level, i.e. the relationship between the parts of a movement (the entire cantata contains 16 movements). Here, each pattern number represents the shape of such a part; if a movement contains e.g. 9 different shapes, the above pattern is applied until the number 9: shape 2 therefore appears four times in this movement, shape 3 three times, etc. Each shape, however, comprises a series of microscopic 'characters'. The sequence of these characters follows the sequence of shapes within the movement. And if you look at the 16 movements of the macroscopic structure, you will discover that, from the third movement onward, all odd-numbered movements contain reprise-like elements that remind us of shapes from previous movements (sometimes, of course, as variations that are possible within the framework of repeating shapes).

This makes it possible to experience time itself on various time levels as an organically growing and branching process. Fractal time that cannot be captured by classical alternatives, be they 'open' or 'closed'.

The second aspect of the formal structure of *Shir hashirim* is that of pitches. While in earlier works (*Kantate nach Meister Eckhart, Litanei für 3 Celli, Dialog mit Haydn*) I had already attempted to question equal temperament, the 'subject' of *Shir hashirim* is clearly the experience of the difference between equally tempered and 'natural' intervals of the spectrum (as far as harmony is concerned). In principle, no mediation is possible between these two manifestations of the interval; hearing pure (perfect) intervals is an experience of quality, while hearing tempered intervals represents the process of reading a quantity-governed tone order generated by culture. The tempered system is the reflection of measuring, weighing modern-day mankind that regards nature merely as material and manipulates its physical environment. The musician experiences this conflict between nature and civilisation, which dominates modern-day society, as the manifest conflict of intonation when it comes to the interpretation of tonal music from the past — especially for works written between the 12th and 18th Centuries. By comparison with the blind routine in the music practice of major orchestras and opera houses (who determine the official music scene), the professional performance techniques of ensembles for old music appear like a rediscovery of interval hearing governed by quality.

Of course, there is also the (usually unconscious) auditive correction of equally tempered intervals — especially when confronted with a 19th-Century work. But especially during the serial stage of new music, the awareness of the difference of pure and tempered intervals was lost to compositional conception and thus led to a merely statistical usage of intervals — just think of Alan Forte's work. On the other hand, a kind of compensation for the reflection upon this difference has been developed through the use of microtonal intervals that is gaining ground at a steady pace. It has to be said, though, that microtonal gradations are considered timbre elements rather than different interval structures (Nicolaus A. Huber, Luigi Nono, Giacinto Scelsi).

The aim of *Shir hashirim* is to enable the physical experience of the difference between pure and tempered intervals. It establishes a harmonic thought whose notational and instrumental practice are based on the tempered system but which nevertheless introduces partial spectrums above the chromatic fundamentals by adding and subtracting pure (that is, integer) intervals to or from the respective (tempered) note and modulating both pitches. What is usually created using a ring modulator, is being composed here. This attempt simply had to lead to a new tonal system with a new interval notation system capable of capturing the vast amount of micro intervals created by addition and subtraction in the most precise way possible.

I must add that this new notation only developed during the long process of writing *Shir hashirim* and that I only started using it in works composed after *Shir hashirim*, such as *Kalligraphien* and *Music to hear*. *Shir hashirim* uses only quarter tone symbols, that is, it still relies on a rather coarse approximation of the intervals intended by the composer. During the rehearsals, there were several instances where I had to correct the intonation of the singers and instrumentalists through singing the originally intended pitches — which led to the natural development of the +/− notation. Today, I realise the need for notating the entire work anew and for adding these auxiliary symbols in almost every measure…

Let us suffice to list the differences between tempered and pure intervals:

the temp. minor second *is, compared to the interval* 16:17	*c.*	5 *cents*	flat
major second	8: 9	4	flat
minor third	5: 6	12	flat
major third	4: 5	14	sharp
fourth	3: 4	2	sharp
augmented fourth	8:11	49	sharp
fifth	2: 3	2	flat
minor sixth	5: 8	14	flat
major sixth	3: 5	12	sharp
minor seventh	4: 9	33	sharp
major seventh	8:15	12	sharp

It appears that the divergence of the 11th harmonic amounts to almost 50 cents — i.e. a quarter tone — with respect to the tritone, and that the difference of the 7th harmonic amounts to 33 cents, which is exactly one sixth of a tone. The divergence of the fifth harmonic, 14 cents, (with a tolerance of 2 to 3 cents, or the amount that allows us to experience differences of fifths in an equally tempered system as 'still pure intervals') is half that of 33 cents, and thus a twelfth of a tone.

This finding triggered the idea to divide a tempered semitone into six tones in order to create intervals that — though still tempered — are six times more precise and thus better suited for correcting ambiguities in the thirds, sevenths, and the tritone, and also capable of representing the 'higher' harmonics (that result from modulations) in a much more precise way.

I chose the simplest symbols possible to avoid cluttering the notation:

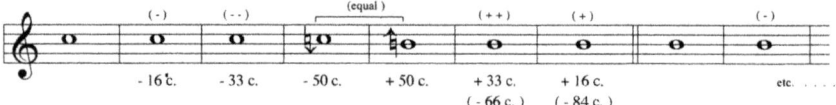

Here is an example of Beethoven's first symphony with my new notation system: (note the quarter-tone difference of the C between measures 2 and 3!)

In *Shir hashirim*, the pitches move as follows: starting from an arbitrary interval, the sum or difference tone is created. (The four resulting pitches can appear either simultaneously or consecutively.) One of these four tones serves as starting point for a new modulation, in which a new — again arbitrarily chosen — pitch added to it creates a new sum and difference. This creates chains that constitute the canvas between the first and the last measures. Here's an example:

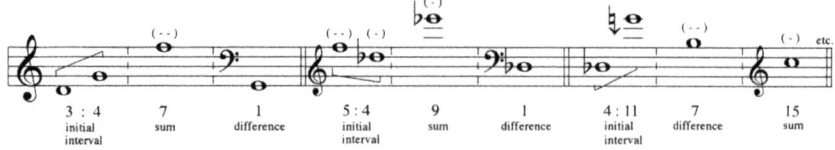

This technique is then expanded in two ways:
1. The modulation process can be continued ad lib thanks to the creation of new sum tones.
Here's an example:

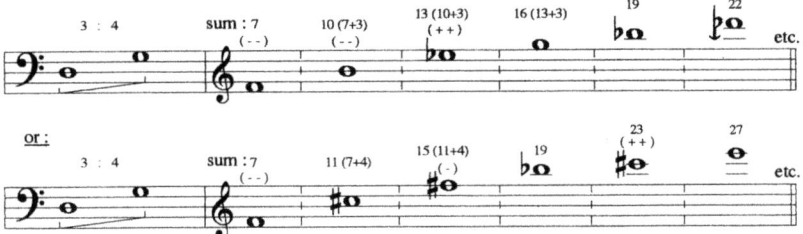

2. One or both of the two tones of the initial interval modulate on a second — randomly chosen — pitch, thus creating multiple modulations, branching on the same trunk.
Example:

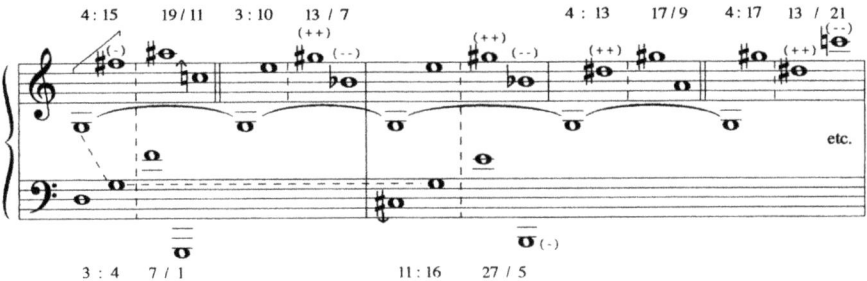

The logically unsolvable problem of the compromise of the harmonic tone series and the equidistant scale, the linearly quantitative thought and the perception of quality appears as paradox in *Shir hashirim*: it is a 'diverging harmony', or, as Heraclitus put it:

παλίντονος ἁρμονίη, ὅκωσπερ τόξου καὶ λύρης.

(diverging combination such as of a bow and a lyre).

Finally, let us have a quick look at my second opera, *Don Quijote* — an in-depth analysis lies beyond the scope of this discussion. With respect to the subject of this paper — the paradoxical union of linear and non-linear thought — the basic concept *Don Quijote* appears to be an extreme example of dealing with non-linearity while preserving linear discipline. The theatrical means: action, pictures, instrumental music, singing, spoken texts, are defined as 5 'parameters'. During the course of the piece, they are combined in several formations, where – according to mathematical law — 31 combinations are possible. That is why *Don Quijote* consists of 31 scenes that represent a new approach of the theatrical possibilities in the guise of 'theatrical adventures'. They 'show' the means of representation (*Darstellung*); using these means and through 'shown' adventures of the absurd hero, they 'show' the perception, both from the point of view of the senses and that of the level of 'making sense' of what is shown, a level that is inextricably linked to the act of perception. The 'trick' of the macroscopic form is to allot the same average duration of 4 minutes (minimum 3, maximum 5) to all 31 scenes, and to 'show' the different perceptions of time when one spends 4 minutes listening to single-part singing, or watching the action on stage supported by the orchestra, or experiencing a radio play in the dark, or watching a set in complete silence with no music or action — or any combination of these basic situations. Staging the most extreme situation — not used in my 31 scenes — of total emptiness, both inaudible and invisible, would lead the listener, or the reader of the present discussion, to him or herself and spark his or her imagination. Allow me therefore to close this discussion on this note.

30.01.'99

PERSONALIAE

NICHOLAS COOK

Nicholas Cook was appointed Professor of Music at the University of Southampton in 1990; from 1996 to 1998 he was Dean of the Faculty of Arts. He is a musicologist and theorist, and previously taught at the Universities of Hong Kong (where he was on the foundation staff of the Department of Music) and Sydney; he was also visiting Professor at Yale University in 1994. He is editor of the "Journal of the Royal Musical Association", and is on the editorial board or advisory panel of other journals including "Music Analysis", "Journal of Music Theory", "South African Journal of Musicology", and "Music Theory Online".

He holds degrees in music and history, and much of his published work has been inter-disciplinary in nature. His books include *A Guide to Musical Analysis*; *Music, Imagination, and Culture Analysis Through Composition*; and a handbook on Beethoven's Ninth Symphony. His articles cover such diverse topics as Beethoven, Liszt, analytical methodology, music in TV commercials, and the aesthetics and psychology of music.

His latest books, both published in 1998 by Oxford University Press, are *Analysing Musical Multimedia* and *Music: A Very Short Introduction*. Oxford also published *Rethinking Music*, a major collaborative volume co-edited by Mark Everist. Current projects include books on Schenker and on the analysis of performance.

Nicholas Cook has been appointed Chair of the Music Panel in the Higher Education Funding Councils' forthcoming Research Assessment Exercise (2001).

PETER JOHNSON

Peter Johnson read Music at Cambridge and took his doctorate from Oxford. His dissertation was on the early atonal repertoire of Schoenberg and Webern. After some years as Professor of Composition in a Brazilian University and lecturer at Kingston Polytechnic (now university), he moved to Birmingham Conservatoire as Head of Undergraduate Studies. He is now Head of Postgraduate Studies and Faculty Research Tutor, and is active in promoting research within the conservatoire community in the UK. He has performed extensively in the UK and abroad as organist, harpsichordist and accompanist and is an accomplished choral director, specialising in the contemporary and pre-reformation repertoires. His current research project concerns the inter-relationships between work and performance.

HANS ZENDER

Hans Zender studied composition (with Wolfgang Fortner), piano, and conducting at the 'Musikhochschulen' in Frankfurt and Freiburg (Germany). After working at the Freiburg Municipal Theatre and a fellowship at Rome's Villa Massimo, he was appointed principal conductor of the Bonn Opera, then General Music Director of the cities of Kiel and Hamburg as well as of the Hamburg State Opera. In 1987, he became the principal conductor of the Radiokamerokest of the Dutch Radio Corporation. Other assignments included an appointment as principal guest conductor of the National Opera in Brussels (Belgium).

Appointed professor for composition at the Frankfurt Musikhochschule in 1988, Zender is also a member of the Akademie der Künste in Berlin as well as of the Bayerische Akademie der Künste Munich. In 1997, he was awarded the Music Prize and the Goethe Prize of the city of Frankfurt.

He is currently the permanent guest conductor and member of the artistic board of the SWR symphony orchestra and guest conductor of various orchestras throughout the world.

The number and quality of his CD and television recordings are as impressive as his compositions (chamber music, orchestral music and vocal works), such as *Stephen Climax*, *Don Quijote* (operas), *Schubert's Winterreise* and *Shir Hashirim*.

He has published two volumes of essays entitled *Happy New Ears* and *Wir steigen niemals in denselben Fluß* (published by Herder, Freiburg). The cpo label has just released a 'Zender Edition' that comprises 17 CDs with works from Mozart to Zender.

EDITORS
Frank Agsteribbe, Peter Dejans

AUTHORS
Nicholas Cook, Peter Johnson, Hans Zender

TRANSLATION
XLNT Communication, Brussels

LAY-OUT
Leopold en Zonen, Ghent

PRESS
Vanmelle, Ghent/Mariakerke
Bioset, 100gr

ISBN 90 6186 994 3
D/1999/1869/56
© 1999 by Leuven University Press / Universitaire Pers Leuven /
Presses Universitaires de Louvain
Blijde-Inkomststraat 5, B-3000 Leuven (Belgium)

All rights reserved.
Except in those cases expressly determined by law,
no part of this publication may be multiplied,
saved in an automated data file or made public in any way whatsoever
without the express prior written consent of the publishers.

www.ingramcontent.com/pod-product-compliance
Ingram Content Group UK Ltd.
Pitfield, Milton Keynes, MK11 3LW, UK
UKHW021834140426
5217IPUK00021B/1446